EVERYDAY
DISCIPLE MAKING

Michael Kramer

CONTENTS

INTRODUCTION

Forty-six years ago, a young man at Purdue University stumbled on a Bible study being conducted by men whose heartbeat and ministry was disciple making. It changed the course of his life and ignited a passion in him to make disciples for Jesus. Twenty-three years later, this man's son would join the same ministry. For the next six years my faith would be challenged and deepened by the Navigators, a para-church ministry that focused on disciple making. At the end of six years my new bride, who had been impacted by the Navigators, and I faced a major crossroads in our lives. We had been asked to join collegiate staff with the Navigators at Purdue University. At the same time, I had been accepted to seminary in Dallas, Texas. Which path would God have us pursue?

Before arriving at this fork in the road, several men, all associated with the Navigators, had already deeply shaped my thinking regarding disciple making. These men were John, Bob VanZante, and Dawson Trotman.[1] The first two men showed me what disciple making looked like in the collegiate world by intentionally investing in me over the course of four years. The latter was the founder of the Navigators, whose recorded talks, biographies, and legacy I discovered in my early twenties. These men were formative to my thinking regarding disciple making. The weight of these men's influence made our decision between collegiate ministries with the Navigators and enrolling in seminary to train for the pastorate very difficult.

As Katherine and I prayed, we thought we understood what para-church ministry would hold. We foresaw by God's grace more fruitful years impacting the lives of college students for Christ. But the call of pastoral ministry was strong and God was opening doors that were scary, risky, and unknown. These were opportunities that would test our faith and expand our horizons. I wanted to preach, and we wanted to impact generations for Jesus. We began to pray. Specifically that God would allow our passion for disciple making to be exported out of the para-church ministry on a college campus and imported back into the Church and broader community. Could this be done? Would God use us?

With this prayer we moved 1,000 miles to Dallas, Texas to begin seminary. We had kids, made a second move to Atlanta, and then a third move to Southern Illinois where God planted us in a loving church family and provided me with a privileged position where I could serve within the Church. After seven years consumed by education and familial life change, I found myself serving where both my setting and co-workers would afford me a unique season of disciple making.

During the previous seven years of transition across four state lines with the advent of four children along the way, the flame of disciple making continued to burn but in hindsight not as brightly as I had wished. The rigors of ministry preparation, constant transitions of life, and in some cases a simple lack of maturity greatly dimmed my flame of disciple making. Yet, looking back there were men whose presence caused the flame of disciple making to brighten and even dance in what one theologian called "The dark night of the soul."

At Dallas Theological Seminary, "Prof." Howard Hendricks thrilled my heart in the classroom. But when he would speak of meeting in the early hours of his busy day with a dozen men each semester, I felt the burden to be engaged in disciple making. Men like Chuck Swindoll, Chip Ingram, and a host of other ministry giants had been influenced by Prof. Would the Lord give me a season to impact men on that scale? The flame flickered. Other men materialized, invested, and influenced: Reed Ashwill, a godly Sunday School teacher who invested beyond the classroom; Thurman Hays and Bryce Norton, pastors who challenged my thinking on evangelism and investing in men; and peers who shared similar heartbeats, Nathan Davis, Jack Kemp, and Tyler Binney. It was the best of times, it was the worst of times, yet the heart beat for disciple making remained.

When we arrived in Southern Illinois, my now senior pastor, Pastor Sammy Simmons, commented at my interview, "We are opposites and therefore I think we will pair well together in ministry." Little did we realize the extent of this truth. It did not take long in the trenches of ministry to realize that our personalities were as different as night and day, but Jesus doesn't make mistakes in his pairings. He has a way of refining, sharpening, and strengthening through differences of personality. While the differences of personality were foreseen, the last seven years we have realized that our two respective ministry heartbeats, evangelism and disciple making, hold the greatest potential for the kingdom impact and possibly the greatest change in our own personal walks with Jesus.

Two years into the pastorate, another fork in my disciple making journey would arise from the encouragement of Pastor Sammy. Much to my surprise, I found myself applying for doctoral work at Southern Seminary. The night of the President's reception the newly matriculated Ph.D. students were told by President Al Mohler, "The next four years will be the most thrilling and arduous you will ever experience." His words would ring true. Yet in this, my second academic journey, the flame for disciple making was fanned. A constant stream of men to invest in materialized. I was being given an opportunity to try, test, and hone a process of disciple making. Meeting with these men at the local diner became my joy and passion in the midst of the combined rigors of ministry and academia.

Yet, still God brought other men to sharpen and guide my course. Men in whose heart beat a passion for disciple making. My Ph.D. advisors Dr. Wilder, Dr. Pennington, and Dr. Pettigrew all valued and championed disciple making. My classmates, who hailed from every corner of the country, sharpened and challenged my ideals of disciple making. My readings were filled with men like Coleman, Ogden,

Gallaty, and Bonhoeffer and continued to stretch my concepts of disciple making.

While the seeds of this book were planted twenty years ago with the Navigators at Purdue University, this book has been the field-testing in the fires of ministry while I have been yoked with Pastor Sammy. As we sat discussing my manuscript in his office, he looked up and commented, "I think maybe we have changed each other more than we realized. I have come to value disciple making more and you have grown in evangelism and missions." At their heart, evangelism and disciple making, rightly understood and applied, do not compete. One flows from the other and both are commanded by God.

Leo Tolstoy stated, "Everyone thinks of changing the world, but no one thinks of changing himself." It seems that in the midst of a journey of two men, both have been changed. Maybe appropriately stated, we are now better centered on Christ. May God now see fit in His infinite wisdom to use this book to change the world, one man or woman at a time.

CHAPTER 1
Who Makes Disciples?

A Curious Conversation

The clock read 6:44 a.m. when I heard the soft knock at my upstairs office door. It was my eight-year-old daughter Sophia. I shifted my Bible to one side of my lap as Sophia climbed up into the chair. We barely fit as she sleepily snuggled up next to me. "Daddy," she said, "Maybe I'll be a missionary some day and share with people about Jesus?" She thought for a second and then she said, "Maybe I'll be a nurse, I could share Jesus as a nurse, too." I chuckled to myself. I have been telling her that nursing is a good profession. "Sweetie, there is more to following Jesus than just sharing the Gospel. We are also called to make disciples. Do you know what it looks like to make a disciple?" Sophia thought for a minute and then surprised me with a very well thought out answer, "We invite people to church, give them a Bible, and share the Gospel with them."

I am biased, but for an eight-year-old, my daughter's answer was very intuitive and logical: a good church, a used Bible, and a willingness to evangelize what more could there be to disciple making? As I pondered her response, it struck me that when it comes to disciple making, most Christians would agree that going to church, promoting the Bible, and sharing the Gospel is disciple making. But, is there more to disciple making? Is this what Jesus meant when He commanded His followers to make disciples in Matthew 28:19-20?[2]

Was Jesus telling them to invite their friends to church? Was Jesus telling them to read their New Testaments in the morning? Was Jesus talking about primarily sharing the good news of His death, burial, and resurrection? Or, was Jesus calling His followers to something that required even more intentionality?

These are important questions that we should not take lightly. If Jesus commands us to "make disciples," we should pay attention. Obedience to Jesus is key to the Christian's life. So we should know exactly what Jesus is talking about, understand why we are doing what we are doing, and lastly we should have a plan on how we will accomplish Jesus' call on our lives. What has He called you and me to do? He has called us to make disciples.

This book explores the who, what, why, when, where, and how of disciple making. It is my prayer that all who read this book are challenged to follow Jesus in whatever way He calls. But it is not enough to just be challenged; we must be willing to take action for the sake of Jesus.

Somewhere in the last 2,000 years we have lost sight of the details of the Great Commission. Jesus' disciples, who heard His last words as recorded in the book of Matthew and then preceded to carry out what is known as the Great Commission, seem to be distant figures of a bygone era. As Christians, we lead extremely busy lives. For most of us as an idea of intentionally investing time to train other men or women to follow Jesus seems foreign. We feel like disciple making is much more applicable to fishermen who followed a Rabbi named Jesus in the distant world of Palestine. We talk of personal evangelism and push personal spiritual growth, but rarely hold up disciple making as the ideal of the Christian life.

As Americans, this is not surprising for we value independence and live in a highly individualistic society. The concept of giving time to intentionally walk alongside another in order to mentor, train, or even coach another individual seems invasive and maybe even a little arrogant. The thought of disciple making brings to mind a host of questions: Who are we to make a disciple? Isn't it the job of the professional pastor to make disciples? What would a disciple maker look like? What would be the end goal?

Often in the evangelical denominations and the Christian academic world, disciple making seems to play second fiddle to evangelism, missions, church planting, church revitalization, or developing leadership skills within the church world. Many view disciple making and evangelism as two separate

entities, which sadly results in disci[
evangelism being pitted against one
evangelism and disciple making are
talked about separately. Consider th
bestow on our church pastors. We h
pastors and evangelism pastors, yet ~~both are~~
commanded to be disciple makers and both are called
to share the Gospel. Actually, Scripture does not
present evangelism and disciple making as mutually
exclusive. Jesus' disciples made disciples (2 Timothy
2:2) and they shared the Gospel (Romans 1:16).
Evangelism is the necessary first step of disciple
making, and disciple makers will actively look to
share his or her faith with the lost.

So, what did Jesus mean when He commanded His
disciples to make disciples? For a clear picture of
disciple making, let's go to the Bible and look at
Jesus' last words in the Gospel of Matthew.

This passage is also referred to as the Great
Commission. For many, the Great Commission is a
new concept. A recent survey conducted by Barna
Research, in conjunction with the Seed Company,
found that 51% of professing Christians have not
heard of the Great Commission. Barna Research
records,

"When asked if they had previously 'heard of the
Great Commission,' half of U.S. churchgoers (51%)
say they do not know this term. It would be
reassuring to assume that the other half who know the
term are also actually familiar with the passage

by this name, but that proportion is low
%). Meanwhile, 'the Great Commission' does ring
a bell for one in four (25%), though they can't
remember what it is. Six percent of churchgoers are
simply not sure whether they have heard this term
'the Great Commission' before.[3]

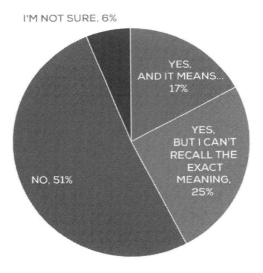

CHURCHGOERS: HAVE YOU HEARD OF THE GREAT COMMISSION?

Barna

I'M NOT SURE, 6%

YES, AND IT MEANS... 17%

YES, BUT I CAN'T RECALL THE EXACT MEANING, 25%

NO, 51%

October 2017, n=1,004 U.S. churchgoers.   © 2018 | barna.com

Let's look together at where the Great Commission
originates. The Great Commission originates from
Jesus' words in Matthew 28:19-20. Jesus states in
Matthew 28:19-20,

> *"Go therefore and **make disciples** of all the nations, baptizing them in the name of the Father and the Son and the Holy Spirit, teaching them to observe all that I commanded you; and lo, I am with you always, even to the end of the age."*

2,000 years ago, Jesus' disciples did not seem confused by His marching orders. They were not commanded to invite people to their synagogue, the Jewish equivalent of a church. They were not commanded to distribute Bibles. They had the Old Testament but there was no New Testament. The New Testament would be written and circulated in pieces over the next 50 years. Jesus' followers would have been well versed in the Old Testament, the Law and the Prophets, which were taught in the Jewish home, read in community at the synagogue, and studied religiously at the temple.

In the Great Commission, Jesus does not specifically command His disciples to evangelize, though this is a necessary part of disciple making. There are many other places in the Bible where followers of Jesus are called to evangelize (e.g. Acts 1:8, Romans 1:16-17, and Mark 16:15).[4] In Matthew 28, Jesus' disciples were commanded to make disciples. So what is disciple making? Let me offer a three-part definition of disciple making:

- Disciple making is an intentional spiritual investment in the life of another believer.

- Disciple making focuses on modeling and teaching another believer how to follow Jesus.
- Disciple making will reproduce followers of Jesus.

If we put these three parts together, we get a working definition of disciple making:

> *Disciple making is an intentional spiritual investment in the life of another believer, which focuses on modeling and teaching how to follow Jesus so that the other believer can replicate other believers who will follow, model, and teach others to follow Jesus.*

This is a broad definition, but most hold too narrow a definition of disciple making. Many view disciple making as the job of the pastor or the "professional" Christian. This limits who is qualified to make disciples. Some believe evangelism equals disciple making. Others view church programming as the key to disciple making. These practical moves limit the depth of disciple making. Often disciple making is relegated to the act of preaching and teaching. This limits how disciples can be made.

This book is designed to challenge the prevalent view of disciple making, and help us to be able to clearly answer the question, "Am I making disciples?" The following chapters will argue that the greatest potential for disciple making is not found in those who are the "professionals." Disciple making is more than evangelism. Disciple making resists programing, and the best context for disciple making is often not found through a 30-minute sermon or weekly Bible study.[5] While the proclamation of the Word within a local congregation is the necessary role of a pastor, the definition for disciple-making given in this book seeks to move beyond preaching, a one-way dialogue, to intentionally investing one's life in two-way dialogue, resulting in life change, spiritual reproduction, and kingdom gain in the life of the disciple. The contrast of the historical ministry impact of George Whitefield and John Wesley is insightful in supporting the ideal of disciple making being more than preaching:

The most significant difference between these two revival preachers is probably the difference in their legacy. George Whitefield is remembered for his intense spiritual life and his loud voice, for telling captivating stories that filled his sermons, for open-air or "field preaching", and for the large numbers of people impacted by his persuasive preaching. All these however died when he did [sic]. Whitefield did not mentor or apprentice revival preachers so there were not individuals who could carry on what he did. His lack of attention to what would survive him is also evident in the handling of the Bethesda orphanage in Savannah Georgia. Although he transferred the patronage to Lady Huntingdon in the UK she did not follow through, so that the institution fell on hard times and had to find its way apart from its benefactor. Whitefield set a high standard of what a revival preacher can do which has inspired others who came after him. Some of his sermons exist however the context into which they were delivered has changed. . . By contrast, the Methodist denomination which sprung up around and after Wesley has over 12 million members at the time of this writing and a long history in the revival awakenings in American history.[6]

Let's pause and ask an important question. "Who is making disciples today?" To answer this question, let us look at four versions of present day disciples of Jesus. We will call them Disciples 1.0, 2.0, 3.0, and 4.0. Let us ask two questions as we look at these 4 versions of disciples. (1) Which disciple of Jesus is making disciples? (2) Which disciple of Jesus am I?

Disciple 1.0 – Spiritual Growth

This first disciple is a follower of Jesus who is taking steps to intentionally grow in their faith. They have accepted Jesus as their Savior and have taken ownership of their personal relationship with Jesus by trying to take steps to follow Jesus.

Our daughter, Sophia is a great example of this type of disciple. Sophia accepted Jesus as her Savior when she was six years old. As a pastor's daughter, she consistently attends church, pays attention during the sermon, engages in Sunday school, and sees church attendance as a highlight of her week. As part of our family, she has been taught how to read her Bible and pray daily. Recently, of her own initiative, she declared to her mom that she was going to read through the Bible. Being the child of parents who consistently seek to share Jesus and being a part of a church with a strong emphasis on evangelism, Sophia has a high sensitivity for others to receive Jesus as Savior.[7]

Understanding Sophia's background, her answer to, "What does it mean to make disciples?" is very logical: (1) invite others to church, (2) give them a Bible, and (3) share the Gospel.[8] Yet, as the character Yoda from Star Wars might say, "A disciple maker you are not." While this conclusion that Sophia is not a disciple maker may seem unfair, as she is only eight, the reality is that the American church is filled with followers of Jesus who never moved past Disciple 1.0.

Many believe that Jesus died on the cross for their sins, but will never follow in His footsteps of making disciples. Some, like Sophia, are even willing to share their faith potentially leading to the birth of spiritual babies BUT are they making disciples of these spiritual babes so that they can make disciples? How are we doing? Are we making disciples? Is Disciple 1.0 our goal? What might Disciple 2.0 look like?

Disciple 2.0 – Spiritual Service

While most of the growing Disciple 1.0's focus lies primarily in private devotion or spiritual disciplines such as: fellowship at church, Bible reading, prayer, and evangelism, Disciple 2.0 builds on this foundation by seeking to intentionally serve inside the church and engage with the Gospel outside of the church. These individuals are the 20% of the church body that get things done. They are servants, givers, teachers, encouragers, exhorters, and leaders. They keep the church as an organization moving forward in its day-to-day and week-to-week ministry. The engaged disciple understands that they have been given a spiritual gift and are not afraid to use it.[9] They understand that their worship of Jesus extends beyond the building up of their own faith, and they will willingly sacrifice their time, energy, and resources to engage in ministry efforts within the church and mission efforts outside the church. These disciples also understand the importance of sharing their faith and have given intentional thought and effort as to how they can share the Gospel with others. What might Disciple 2.0 look like?

A couple weeks ago, I had a dear friend from college drop by while he was traveling on a business trip. I have known him for almost twenty years. I have been able to watch his life through different seasons of his journey, and I know that he loves Jesus. I watched him own his faith in a Bible study during our college days. I know that he leads his family to faithfully attend church and models for them what it means to love Jesus. He reads his Bible, prays, and is committed to sharing his faith. As we caught up, he shared how he has been leading a small group class at his church, had been praying about becoming part of a church plant supported by his church, and we even discussed some of the issues he had been facing as he tries to offer leadership and guidance within his church. I love my friend and he loves Jesus and Jesus' Church. He is an engaged disciple.

As we chatted, I shared some thoughts about this book. As we talked about disciple making, he made the comment, "I am not making disciples." One of my friend's strengths is his honesty and willingness to self-examine. On paper, he is doing all the right things in his private and public devotional life, but in his mind, he is not making disciples. As he left, I felt the weight of our conversation. I wondered to myself, if Disciple 2.0 is not making disciples, does this mean that disciple making is not happening in the pews? Is disciple making unintentionally being left to the pastor, or the professional? Is it just those who have been called to ministry who are responsible to make disciples? Let us now turn to Disciple 3.0, the ministry professional.

Disciple 3.0 – Pastoral

I must make a disclaimer at the beginning of this section. The analogy of Disciple 1.0, 2.0, and 3.0 is good but begins to break down at Disciple 3.0. All stand equal before the cross. All are called to be intentionally growing in their faith and engaged in the body of Christ. Yet, some are uniquely called as ministers of the Gospel. In our culture this usually means, potentially pursuing additional education, entering a vocational or co-vocational ministry, and becoming recognized as a "professional."

Whatever the title, Pastor, Minister . . . Reverend, or

Doctor, Ephesians 4:11-12 states the purpose of the pastor and the saints,

> *And He gave some as apostles, and some as prophets, and some as evangelists, and some as pastors and teachers, **for the equipping of the saints for the work of service** [emphasis added], to the building up of the body of Christ.*

Pastors (and teachers) are to equip the saints to do the work of service, which is the building up of the body of Christ. Does this mean that the pastor is the only one to make disciples? Pastors, as followers of Jesus, do fall under the command of Matthew 28:19-20, but placing the responsibility of the disciple making solely on the shoulders of one specific pastor or the pastoral staff will greatly limit the potential for disciple making.

A dedicated pastor's job description tends to be quite lengthy. At the top of the list for most congregations is preaching and leadership. If your church is located in a more rural setting, pastoral shepherding such as counseling, hospital runs, and home visits, hold an even greater value for the congregation.

Complementing these primary expectations of preaching and shepherding are a litany of other diverse responsibilities. This should not be a surprise. If disciple making is not highly valued or articulated by the church body, it is doubtful that it will happen.

Without an intentional plan disciple making will simply not happen.[10]

If you are reading this as a pastor, you may be thinking. I make disciples while I am preaching or giving direction to the church. Yes, there is validity in this thought, but if we are honest we must be willing to ask, "How much disciple making takes place in a one-way conversation from the pulpit, time spent studying in our office, or giving direction from the lead seat in a boardroom?" Deep down we know that, disciple making is caught, not taught. If we have been in ministry long enough, we also suspect that the best disciple making resists programming and is instead deeply personal. After all, did Jesus have a pulpit, study, or boardroom? Jesus did preach to the crowds, but there was something greater taking place during the intentional time Jesus invested in the twelve. Disciples were being made.

A Disciple Making Journey

I first experienced disciple making in my home growing up. My parents believed that it was their responsibility, not the church's, to ensure my spiritual formation. I first actively participated in disciple making during college through the disciple making ministry of the Navigators. But it was not until my late twenties and early thirties when I experienced two dramatic changes in my life that I really began to focus on disciple making. First, I became a parent. Second, I became a pastor. Suddenly the question of disciple making became deeply personal. I was forced to ask the question, "What does it mean for me to make disciples?"

As a parent, was disciple making something more than insuring my kids were in a solid church? I have watched too many good kids, raised in church by well-meaning parents and grandparents, walk away from Jesus as young adults.

As a pastor, I had other questions. What are we as pastors asking our people in the pew to do? Is our goal Disciples 1.0, 2.0, and 3.0, and are these disciples reproducing themselves by making disciples? Whose job is it to make disciples: the professionals, the church and church programming, individual Christians, or a combination of all?

\ Christian educator, I had questions. Does \ch programming make disciple makers or do people make disciple makers? What type of disciple (1.0, 2.0, or 3.0) does church programing produce?

Now please don't get me wrong. I want my kids in church. As a pastor, my kids have pretty good church attendance. Do not mistake my questions surrounding the church and disciple making as a lack of love for the Church. I love the Church and am deeply committed to the local church. Jesus loves the Church with all its bumps and bruises, and so will I. Jesus died for the Church and is coming back for the Church. Your church is an amazing gift designed to grow your walk with Jesus. It is a greenhouse where our faith can deepen, grow, and bloom. I am also not advocating getting rid of church programming.

Programming can be helpful as far as it achieves the intended. Church programming (consisting of Bible study, fellowship, and evangelistic events) is a useful tool, but will attendance and programming alone produce disciple makers? This brings me back to Sophia's answer of (1) invite to church, (2) give Bibles, and (3) share the Gospel. Is disciple making something more? Is there a Disciple 4.0?

What follows is what I am learning about disciple making. I use the word learning, as the following chapters are not exhaustive or perfect and the application of disciple making in my life is being continually refined. There is no cookie cutter approach to disciple making, but there are certain ingredients that make disciple making more successful. In chapter 2, we will seek to answer the question, "What is disciple making?" As we look deeper into Scripture, we will find that God's Word provides a clear blue-print for disciple making. Specifically, Jesus' and his disciples' example for what disciple making might look like in our lives.

In the next chapter we will look at what disciple 4.0 might look like.

CHAPTER 2
What is Disciple Making?

As I sat in the coffee shop, I did my best not to eavesdrop on a conversation taking place between a father and his son at the table catty-corner from me. Trying to not listen in but instead focus on final preparation for my Ph.D. seminar presentation due in 30 minutes, I realized that they were talking about the Bible and life. I could not help myself. I walked over and interrupted their conversation. After a brief introduction, I looked at the young boy and said, "You are fortunate to have a dad that intentionally spends time with you. That is awesome!" He bashfully grinned. I turned to his dad and asked, "Where did you learn to meet with your son like this? Did your dad do this with you when you were a kid?"

A peculiar look came over his face, "No." He paused, thinking reflectively, "My dad was a great dad and a godly Christian man, but he was too busy with other responsibilities to be able spend time with me like this. He was a great dad, but we didn't do this."

Sometimes we miss great things, like investing

spiritually in the lives of our kids or others that God
has placed around us. Most don't know how to begin.
Maybe they have never thought of disciple making.
Perhaps they have thought about it, and the thought
makes them fearful so they never take steps to make
disciples. Maybe they have never seen disciple
making modeled.

It is worth noting that the idea of disciple making,
that is spiritually investing or mentoring another
person is not a foreign concept to the New Testament.
In fact the opposite is true as the New Testament is
full of disciple making. Paul in his closing statements
to the church in Philippi writes,

> *The things you have learned and received and*
> *heard and seen in me, practice these things,*
> *and the God of peace will be with you.*
> (Philippians 4:9)

Paul did more than preach. He taught, transmitted,
and modeled ("you have … received and heard and
seen"). In a word, Paul trained others.

Ultimately disciple making begins in the home. But
disciple making must also be modeled in the church
and this begins with pastors. Those in the pew will
never surpass the example set by those leading from
the front. Disciple making is caught, not taught.
Disciple making is not a program; it is a lifestyle.

As pastors we, like Paul, must be willing to model
disciple making to those who are looking to our

example. If you are a pastor you probably feel overwhelmed by the thought of adding something to your already overflowing calendar. Let us put this in perspective. As a pastor, if you commit to making disciples; it will cost you time. You will have to make a conscious decision to engage in disciple making. By my experience it will cost you in time 2-3 hours a week or about 5% of your work.

Can you afford to not model disciple making? If the answer is no, I challenge you to pray about committing 5% of your time to disciple making. You will find that this 5% will be some of your sweetest time in ministry. You also may begin a God-size movement that will impact your church beyond your next sermon or decisions you make at your next meeting. While you are constrained by the necessity of preaching and leading, what good thing on your calendar can you trade for a great thing like disciple making?

What made me so excited about what I saw in the coffee shop? I was witnessing disciple making taking place. I had found a disciple maker 4.0. In this chapter we will identify 3 biblical ingredients to disciple making and offer a comprehensive definition for disciple making.

So who or what is disciple maker 4.0? Let's look again at our definition of a disciple making.

Disciple making is an intentional spiritual investment in the life of another believer, which focuses on modeling and teaching how to follow Jesus so that the other believer can replicate other believers who will follow, model, and teach others to follow Jesus.

Let us break this definition of disciple making from Matthew 28:19-20 into three parts.

- Disciple making is an intentional spiritual investment in the life of another believer
- Disciple making focuses on modeling and teaching another believer how to follow Jesus.
- Disciple making will reproduce followers of Jesus who reproduce.

We will now look at the first of the three ingredients that go into disciple making: intentionally investing in the life of another.

Disciple Making is an Intentional Spiritual Investment in the Life of Another Believer

Disciple making requires time. Disciple making does not typically take place in an hour on Sunday morning. Disciple making is not a brief conversation, a passing encounter, or something that can be transmitted in the class-room. Disciple making requires time, like time spent by a father with a son in a coffee shop.

Time has always been a premium. To want for more time is to be human. Yet, Jesus made an intentional time investment over three years in the lives of twelve men.[11] Jesus was a carpenter, and they were fishermen. He was thirty and they were probably younger than him. They were normal guys and Jesus was their Rabbi.

As a Jewish Rabbi, Jesus assumed the role of teacher, but His teaching context was much different than the classroom setting that we typically ascribe to a teacher. Jesus preached to the crowds, impacted communities, but ultimately He invested his most focused attention in twelve men. Jesus walked with His disciples. He did life with His disciples. Jesus, using modern day descriptors, was more of a mentor, life-coach, and a very intentional friend than a small group facilitator, Sunday school teacher, or preacher. Jesus' calling card found in Matthew 4:19 was, "Come follow me and I will make you fishers of men." Was Jesus' method of fishing for men unique for Him as the Son of God or could His example of intentional spiritual investment in others be what it takes to make disciples?

Let's look at the apostle Paul, writer of three-fourths of the New Testament and formerly known as Saul. Saul was a Pharisee, religion was his profession. He was educated and had political influence. Paul was on a meteoric rise to power and position within the Jewish religious establishment of the day and on a personal vendetta to stamp out the cult of Christianity, which was encroaching on Judaism.

Saul meets Jesus and becomes Paul with a new commission of taking the Gospel to the Gentiles.

On Paul's first mission trip, he takes Barnabas and John Mark as traveling companions. Later Paul takes Silas. In Corinth Paul meets Aquila and Priscilla. Afterward Aquila and Priscilla invest in a man named Apollos. Paul mentors Timothy. He also coaches another young man named Titus. There are others that he invests in who did not continue to follow Jesus. Not only did Paul share the Gospel with Gentiles and plant churches, Paul made intentional spiritual investments in the lives of others whether traveling, living in a major metropolitan center like Ephesus, or spending time in jail. Paul followed the example of Jesus: Paul made intentional spiritual investments in individuals.

You may wonder whether Jesus' disciples followed Jesus' example in disciple making in the early church. They did. Tradition holds that the Apostolic Fathers (Clement of Rome, Ignatius of Antioch, Polycarp of Smyrna, and Papias of Hierapolis and others) were trained by the Twelve. Since many of these giants of the faith were martyred; it's safe to say that they were committed to the cause of Christ.

The Greek Fathers: Justin Martyr, Irenaeus of Lyons, Clement of Alexandria, Athanasius of Alexandria, John Crysostom, and Curil of Alexandria and the Cappadocian Fathers: Basil of Caesarea, Gregory Nazianzus, Peter of Sebaste, Gregory of Nyssa, Maximus the Confessor, and John of Damascus would have been second and third generation disciples of the Apostolic Fathers.

Other third and fourth generation disciples would include the Latin Fathers (Gregory, Ambrose, Augustine, and Jerome) and the Syriac Fathers. All had a profound impact on Christianity providing guidance to the early church and combating heresy that threatened to corrupt Jesus Christ's teachings.

Unless you are a church historian, you may not recognize most of the names above. You may recognize examples in more recent Christian history of those who made intentional spiritual investments in others. It is reported that Martin Luther often hosted 12-20 men at his dinner table every Sunday for lunch. He started a disciple making movement that swept through Germany and spilled into Europe. Disciple making was the catalyst for the beginning of the Reformation. Ultimately, Luther's followers in Germany would form a denomination known as Lutheranism.[12]

The Fathers of our modern day missionary movement were disciple makers. Adoniram Judson, William Cary, Hudson Taylor (Myanmar, India, and China respectively) all made disciples that created Christian movements.

Now you and I may not be used by God to start a disciple making movement that turns into a denomination or to develop a Christian movement on a faraway soil. But disciple making is always at the center of any season in church history or any place in the world where Christianity is burning the brightest. We should not be surprised.

The principle of disciple making is laid out in Scripture and Jesus' specific command to His disciples was to intentionally spiritually invest in others so that they could make disciples. What would be a practical application for us as pastors, lay-leaders, and congregants? Maybe we should stop praying for revival in America and go make some disciples. Who knows, maybe we would influence the next Wesley or Whitefield.[13]

Don't forget disciple makers impacted men like Jonathan Edwards (his father, Timothy Edwards, his mother, Esther Stoddard, and elder sisters), D.L. Moody (Edward Kimball), Billy Sunday (J. Wilbur Chapman), and Billy Graham (Henrietta Mears). You might say to yourself, this is all good and grand, but I am no one special. You are absolutely correct, but neither were the men and women listed above (Jesus being the obvious exception). Moody's famous statement rings true, "The world has yet to see what God will do with a man fully consecrated to him."[14]

These followers of Jesus took His command to make disciples seriously. God did the rest. John 15:5 states,

I am the vine, you are the branches; he who abides in Me and I in him, he bears much fruit, for apart from Me you can do nothing.

What about you and me? We are Christ's followers. We have been commanded to make disciples. Do we have two hours a week (outside of Sunday morning) where we can intentionally spiritually invest in another individual? Can you think of someone in your life with whom you could make an intentional spiritual investment?

Disciple making is more than your devotional life and Sunday morning worship. Disciple making is more than private, public, or professional worship. Again, don't get me wrong, reading your Bible and prayer are essential, but you are feeding yourself. Being part of the community of faith is commanded, but on Sunday morning you are the one who is being blessed. Preaching and shepherding are a high calling, but the majority of pastoral work involves dealing with people's issues, prepping for sermons, programming, and overseeing a church budget. These are all good, necessary, and excellent things, but are they disciple making?

You may be wondering if involvement in discipleship programs at church or in the community makes you a disciple. We must make a distinction between participating in a discipleship activity and disciple making. What distinguishes being engaged in discipleship from disciple making? Engaging in discipleship is about you. Making a disciple is about someone else.

In 2 Timothy 2:2 Paul directs young Timothy,

> *The things which you have heard from me in the presence of many witnesses, entrust these to faithful men who will be able to teach others also.*

Similarly, in Titus chapter 2, Paul encourages Titus and his flock to intentionally invest in others. Titus was to instruct those under his pastoral care to make disciples. Titus is exhorted to instruct older men and older women to *"teach . . . encourage"* younger men and women. Titus was to also instruct younger men and women to be *"an example of good deeds . . . and purity of doctrine."* This leads to the second ingredient of disciple making.

Disciple Making is Focused on Modeling and Teaching Another Believer How to Follow Jesus

The second ingredient of disciple making is modeling and teaching another believer how to follow Jesus. 2 Timothy 2:2, Titus 2, and Matthew 28:19-20 all make specific mention of "teaching" or modeling our faith. This central idea of teaching when coupled with modeling moves us beyond Sophia's description of disciple making (give Bible, invite to church, share Gospel).

Most Christians can identify individuals in their life who model what it means to be a Christ follower. When I was boy, there was a godly deacon named Bruce Craig. As a kid, I watched Bruce's life, how he participated in worship, loved his wife, and served his family and his church family. I was not the only one watching. My dad would often talk of Bruce, his wise life decisions, and how he ordered his life. Bruce's conduct honored Christ. Bruce was a godly man and an excellent role model, but he never intentionally taught me.

Most Christians can identify individuals in their life who taught them what it means to be a Christ follower. This might be a faithful pastor, wise Sunday School teacher, or a skilled small group leader. As a newlywed and seminary student, I loved to listen to the gifted preacher Charles Swindoll, on the radio, and I never missed an opportunity to hear him speak at a chapel service at Dallas Theological Seminary. Boy, he could preach the Word, and I found that his personal stories always left me in tears as they would sink down into my heart.

Dr. Swindoll was a powerful preacher and his preaching ministry blessed me. He was an excellent teacher, but I never knew him well enough for him to model his own spiritual life to me in a personal way. Chuck Swindoll was an excellent preacher and he taught me, but he never intentionally modeled his walk with Jesus for me outside of a thirty-minute sermon.

Let us revisit the father and son in the coffee shop. When I interrupted their conversation, they were working through a book by Ken Sande called the *Peace Maker*. When I asked them what they were doing during their weekly time together, the dad responded that they were discussing what they had been reading in the Bible, talking about life circumstances, and whenever they find a relevant book to their current spiritual walks they spend time working through it together.[15] While many things are better caught then taught, this father was not just hoping that his faith would be caught by his son; he was both modeling and teaching him what it looked like to follow Jesus.

Few Christians can identify individuals in their life who made an intentional spiritual investment in their lives while focusing on *both* modeling and teaching them how to follow Jesus. In college, I met a man named Bob. I watched how Bob lived his life. I would see him at our church, the small group Bible study that we led together, and interact with him in the campus ministry that we were both part of. I spent time with Bob around his dinner table, in coffee shops, and on the campus. But Bob did more than model how to follow Jesus. He also met with me each week and taught me what it meant to be a follower of Christ. Bob challenged me in areas of obedience, pushed me to read my Bible, and modeled how to memorize Scripture. He taught me how to share the Gospel and modeled how to live selflessly. I listened as Bob prayed, shared his struggles and fears, and recounted God's faithfulness in his life. I watched how Bob ordered his life, loved his wife, interacted with his kids, treated people, and engaged in church. Bob was *focused on modeling and teaching me how to follow Jesus.* Bob was intentional to teach me how to follow Jesus, but more than this he was modeling and teaching me how to intentionally invest in others. This brings us to the last part of our definition of disciple making.

Disciple Making Will Reproduce Followers of Jesus

Remember the third part of our definition for disciple making? "Disciple making will reproduce followers of Jesus." Why the goal of replication? To answer this, let's look closer at Jesus' last earthly command to His followers found in Matthew 28:19-20, also known as the Great Commission.
Looking closely at the definition of disciple making and replication, disciple making should be understood through the lens of Jesus' Great Commission in Matthew 28:19-20. Jesus gave this command before His ascension.

> *Go therefore and* **make disciples** *[emphasis added] of all the nations, baptizing them in the name of the Father and the Son and the Holy Spirit, teaching them to observe all that I commanded you; and lo, I am with you always, even to the end of the age.*

If you dig into the Greek there is only one command in the entire passage: make disciples. Go, baptizing, and teaching are all participles (action verbs that end in "ing.)" In the sentence structure of the original language all the force lies on the imperative (command) verb *metheteuo*: to make disciples.[16] A literal rendering would be, "[you] *make* disciples…". Going, baptizing, and teaching describe what should be done while we are making disciples. A closer translation of the original language would be,

> *As you are going, make disciples of all nations, baptizing them . . . teaching them to observe all I have commanded you . . .*

So what does a closer look at the original text of Jesus' last command tell Christians to do?

1. "Make disciples." Christ's disciples are commanded to make disciples. They are commanded to replicate.

2. "As you are going…" points to the nature of discipleship. Disciple making is to be part of our DNA, a lifestyle, and a purposeful endeavor as we go about our everyday lives.

3. "Baptizing them…" ties disciple making securely into the context of the Church. Disciple makers and those they are discipling are to be integrated into the local church. As mentioned before, the church is to be a greenhouse for a believer's faith. Baptism also points to the necessity for followers

of Christ to be actively sharing the Gospel. Evangelism is often the first step of disciple making. Those that are baptized must first have a saving relationship with Jesus. Evangelism and engagement in a local body are necessary parts of disciple making.

4. "Teaching them…" centers disciple making on Jesus and the Word of God. We are to train (coach, mentor, disciple, walk alongside) others to understand God's will for our lives as found in His Word.[17] Disciple making is to be centered on both the Word of God, and the object of our affections, Jesus.

So what are the ingredients of disciple making? They are (1) an intentional spiritual investment in the life of another (2) to teach another to follow Jesus (3) so that they can reproduce.

If we put these three ingredients together, we will be faithful to live out Jesus' command to make disciples. We will become disciple maker 4.0 who reproduces followers of Jesus by engaging people in our everyday lives, seeking to connect them to a Bible-teaching, God-honoring church, and then showing them how to grow in their faith so that they will fall deeply in love with Jesus, become more like Jesus, and reproduce other followers of Jesus.[18]

Ultimately the Great Commandment drives the Great Commission. The Great Commandment simply put is, "Love God and love others." The Great

Commission (Matt. 28:19-20 – "Make Disciples") calls us to love others enough to help them better love God. Disciple makers teach others to fall in love with Jesus and obey His Word, which is Jesus' love language (see John 14:21). Disciple making (the Great Commission) therefore reinforces the Great Commandment. This brings us to the why of disciple making. In the next chapters we will look at the "why" and the "why not" of disciple making. We will discover that it is our love for God that propels us as Jesus' followers to love others enough to engage in their lives.

CHAPTER 3
Why Should I Make Disciples?

My alarm went off at 5:15 Thursday morning. It was still dark outside. I reached for my phone to turn my alarm off. My wife, who usually gets up before me, rolled over and continued sleeping peacefully. It was the middle of the week and I had taught our Wednesday night service the night before so I felt more tired than normal. As I showered and quietly dressed, I contemplated why I was up so early on a Thursday morning. In 30 minutes, I would be sitting with three other men at a local diner. Our goal would be to walk through several chapters in the Bible that each in the group had committed to read several times during the previous week. We would spend time praying, review Bible verses that we had memorized the week before, and we would share how Jesus was working in our lives. Our goal was to fall deeper in love with Jesus, grow in maturity, and see new groups form out of our group. My personal goal for each man that I invest in is that they individually would catch a vision for meeting and investing in other men.

I grabbed my car keys, I wondered, "Would these men catch the vision of replication?" I've met with many men around the Word over a cup of coffee, but not all catch the heart to replicate. Many will invest in their own spiritual walk, but few are committed to invest in the lives of others.

As I pondered, I wished I had that cup of coffee now. Getting up at 5:15 to meet with men to pursue Jesus at 6 a.m. is not always easy. There are some mornings that I wonder why I make the effort? Meetings like these often make me feel anxious. I'm an introvert and when life is full or I am stressed people don't energize me. The three guys that I would soon be circled up with were all almost a decade younger than me and all in a different life season then I was. I wondered if I would connect with them in a meaningful way? Would our discussion be relevant to their lives? Would God use this intentional spiritual investment in their lives and would He use these men in my life to sharpen and push me? I mused to myself, "Maybe the Lord was already using them to push me."

Jesus never said that disciple making would be easy. In life, good things don't come easily. They take time, commitment, and effort. Before we investigate how to make disciples we must understand the why of disciple making. Why should you and I expend energy, give time, and risk making disciples?

Below we will walk through five reasons for making disciples. The five reasons are: disciple making (1) is commanded by Jesus, (2) is the pattern given in Scripture, (3) secures the next generation, (4) leads to maturity, and (5) brings purpose beyond self.[19]

Disciple Making is Commanded

As followers of Christ, disciple making is not an option. Disciple making is a command. The Christian life, at its heart, is about submission and obedience to Christ. As discussed in chapter 2, we are commanded in Matthew 28 to make disciples. Jesus states, "He who has my commands and keeps them, he it is who loves me . . .." (John 14:21) Jesus commands us to "make disciples." If we love Jesus, we will keep Jesus' commandments.

Jesus calls us to do what He himself does. Jesus modeled disciple making and His disciples followed His example. Jesus' command in Matthew 28 extends beyond His 12 disciples. Jesus' command is for an audience that is wider than just the professional pastor and those who have been called to the mission field. Disciple making is to be a normative part of the everyday life of all who claim to be followers of Jesus.

Did you catch it? Making disciples is part of being a follower of Christ. Disciple making, like many things in the Christian life, is an issue of obedience. There is joy found in obedience. It is in the midst of obedience that God can bless. God cannot bless where we refuse to obey. Yet, being commanded is not always the most captivating motivation.

If disciple making is not easy, then our motivation to

make disciples must be solid. We must agree that Jesus wants us to make disciples. It is not enough to merely give mental assent, we must take action. Disciple making is a choice, a choice of obedience. This reason alone should be enough to lead us to make disciples. Yet there are other reasons. Why else should we make disciples beyond Jesus' command? We should make disciples because it is the example we find in the Bible.

Disciple Making is the Biblical "Norm"

Jesus made disciples. The 11 apostles made disciples. Paul made disciples. Even though disciple making is modeled in Scripture, it is not easy. Jesus focused on twelve men for three years. One betrayed Him. The rest fled at Jesus' greatest moment of need. The apostle Paul also invested in men. Paul's commentary regarding the men that he had invested in is bleak: "At my first defense, no one came to my support, but everyone deserted me. May it not be held against them" (2 Timothy 4:16). I wonder, did Paul take consolation in the fact that all abandoned Jesus too? The apostles invested in men, some were men like Stephen who was willing to die for his faith. But, I am sure that there were many others who claimed to follow Christ, but when the chips were down abandoned their first love to give themselves to other things. People will disappoint.

I met with a man for six months. He was faithful, available, and I thought he was teachable. As we spent time together, this young man was faithful to read his Bible, memorizing scripture, and attend church. He never missed our weekly meeting. Then one day, after I had invested in him for six months, he sat down across from me and would not look at me. I asked him if he was okay? He said yes but still would not look me in the eyes. I asked him what was bothering him? He then looked at me sheepishly and said, "I have a girlfriend." "Great," I responded, "what's her name?"

My response was generous. This man had experienced lots of broken relationships and was fresh off a recent divorce. Women (a blessing in the right context) were his weakness. As we got to know each other and he shared from his life experiences, I had encouraged him to follow Jesus for a season while growing deeper in his identity in Christ before he pursued the opposite sex. I assured him that in the right time, as he grew and honored the Lord, that God was capable of growing him toward wholeness in an area of life in which he had never had peace. Eventually, if it was the Lord's will He could provide a godly Christian wife. This discussion had come up often over our time together. While I was disappointed that he had not followed what I had thought to be sound advice, there was no sin in having a girlfriend. Perhaps she would be a positive influence, and the Lord would use her to help him grow in his faith?

He shared her name and then commented: "She moved in with me last week." What I had hoped was a good thing had just become a serious issue. Sex outside of marriage is sin, and sexual sin will always stunt spiritual growth. I looked at my friend cautiously and gently said, "You know this isn't right." He shook his head yes. What was he going to do? His response was not promising. A week later, I met with him again. He was going to continue living with his girlfriend. This time, I was ready with my response. I told him that I loved him, but that I did not think now would be the best time to continue to meet as he had a lot on his plate. Maybe in another season we could meet when he was ready to be all in pursuing Jesus. My friend seemed relieved and agreed. I prayed for him, paid for breakfast, and we parted ways. My heart was heavy. The disappointment was real!

Over the next couple of months my friend stopped going to church. I would see him at church on Christmas and maybe Easter. We always smile and shake hands. We like each other. I care for him and love him as a fellow brother in Christ, but he is not pursuing Jesus. A year later, I heard he had buckled under the stress of life. I met with him again and challenged him to follow Jesus, not things or relationships that will never bring the satisfaction that his heart longs for. He received my comfort, but no pursuit of Jesus followed. If people can disappoint, why make disciples?

I met John my sophomore year of college when I showed up at his dorm room and asked if I could share about Jesus with him. I was being trained how to share the Gospel and my mentor and I were following up spiritual surveys collected during freshman orientation at Purdue University with the hope of having the opportunity to share the Gospel (remember, evangelism is part of being a disciple and making disciples).

John answered the door and invited us into his small, dark room. John was sick and looked like he had just been run over by a Mac truck. Against my better judgment we accepted his invitation and sitting on his bed, I nervously butchered a presentation of the Gospel, but God was already at work in John's life. John had been praying and reading his Bible for several months. That day, John asked questions, and I tried to answer his questions.

We left his room and, relieved, I laughed about my rough presentation of the Gospel. My personality will probably never enjoy what I call "cold turkey" evangelism and in hindsight I could have been better prepared to communicate the Gospel, but I had been a faithful disciple and shared. We prayed and moved on.

Had I made a disciple? No, I had shared the Gospel. I was trying to be a disciple evidenced by my willingness to participate in "cold turkey" evangelism. I was part of the disciple making process. A godly Christian man who was quite a bit ahead of me in his walk with Jesus was taking time to meet with me and invest in my spiritual development. So if disciple making is more than evangelism what does disciple making look like?

Two days after I knocked on John's door, I met him by the fountain in the middle of the campus. I was nervous and was not very confident about what I was doing. There I sat with John and shared the Gospel again, a little more clearly this time. He had already accepted Christ on his own. I affirmed his new belief, discussed eternal security, encouraged him to begin reading his Bible, and invited him to join me for church the next week. He overslept the first week. I invited him again and he joined me the second week. Had I made a disciple? No, I had shared the Gospel, talked about eternal security, encouraged John to read the Bible and attend church. Sound vaguely familiar: share the Gospel, give them a Bible, and invite them to church.

But I did more than invite John to church. I encouraged him to begin reading in his Bible (starting with the book of John) WITH ME. I was not seminary trained, I had never been a pastor, had never been married, had kids, or even held a full time job. How did I know to do this? I had seen disciple making modeled. Someone had invested in me.

Over the coming weeks I began to meet with John. I sat with John as he prayed his first audible prayers. More sincere prayers were never heard, "Hi, God. This is John…" I challenged him to memorize Scripture and introduce him to a Christian fellowship where he could make Christian friends. Our disciple making journey had begun. In the coming weeks and months we talked about our lives: backgrounds, families, and areas where we struggled to follow

Christ. We read the Bible together. We spent time together. We pursued Jesus, together! It has been seventeen years since John came to Christ. I was afforded the privilege to invest in John for the first five years of his spiritual life. Other Christians had profound impact on his life, too. Recently, John has been accepted for Medical Residency. I couldn't be prouder. He married a godly Christian woman and has two young kids. He is faithfully engaged in church. When I asked John if I could use his story, he responded "Absolutely, but we may serve as missionaries in a closed country someday so would you mind changing my name?" John is walking with Jesus.

Why make disciples? Because Jesus uses people to change people's lives.

People can be the source of great heartache and great joy! I would not trade the opportunity I had to invest in John for anything. Investing in John has been one of the highlights of my Christian life. By God's grace, I was able to make a disciple. I still pray for John. Though we are miles away and lifetimes apart, one of my prayers for John is that he finds the joy of spiritual reproduction.

Disciple Making Secures the Next Generation

Disciple making does not come naturally; it takes vision, intentionality, and a plan.

In writing this book, I asked my dad who

intentionally invested in me, to share his perspective on disciple making. While my dad does not hold a seminary degree, he has made disciple making a consistent part of his life since college and has decades of experience investing in men from the vantage point of a church member. I found his following thoughts to be very insightful.

Each generation is just one generation away from spiritual dullness and deadness. Just because the current generation is strong and healthy, if we do not raise up and train the next generation, there may be a spiritual desert in the next few years. History is filled with examples of vibrant generations of spiritual progress, only to be followed by spiritual decline because the next generation was not trained to take the torch forward.[20]

The Second Great Awakenings in America saw unprecedented spiritual fervor, only to be followed by decades of spiritual decline. People came to Christ during that time, but foundations of disciple making were not established... just new converts. England saw dramatic spiritual life and growth under the influence of the Wesley brothers [John and Charles], only to be followed by dramatic spiritual decline in the next generation. London was temporarily 'sanctified' under Spurgeon's incredible ministry, but after Spurgeon, London has never seen the same level of spiritual interest. For all intents and purposes, England is spiritually dead today.

> So why make disciples? To ensure the next
> generation remains spiritually strong. Every
> major league team has a farm club developing
> the next generation. If they don't, their team
> will surely decline in just a few short years.
> There always needs to be new blood coming
> to the top. Disciple making is Christianity's
> 'farm club'. It prepares the next generation to
> carry the torch.[21]

Let me give you a very real example illustrating my
dad's point. Just because my dad intentionally
invested in my spiritual development doesn't mean
that his grandkids or great-grandkids will walk with
Jesus or be disciple makers. I will be the first to
acknowledge that it will only be by God's grace that
his grandkids and great-grandkids will walk with
Jesus, but as the generation between him and them, I
am trying to do everything I can to pass the torch of
walking with Jesus to my kids. Yet my end goal is
not that they just walk with Jesus; I want them to
reproduce spiritually for the sake of the Kingdom.
"Judah, let's go out on the porch. We are going to
talk about what it means to be a man." While this
statement might strike you as a little presumptive or
make the edges of your mouth twitch upward, my son
who was nine, was all for it and quickly dashed off to
the porch. For the last year and a half, Judah and I
have been spending intentional father-son time
together after his three younger siblings go to bed.

This ritual does not happen every night and we usually do not spend a long time together – but enough time to wrestle, to play ten or twelve moves of our ongoing chess game, to simply watch the cars go by on the main street of our small town. Tonight, I had decided to up the ante and do more than chat about the day.

As Judah raced away I silently thought to myself, "Well now you've committed yourself, what are you going to tell him? You had better keep it simple; he's only nine." A second after sitting down, Judah looked at me and said, "Ok Dad, I'm ready!" I swallowed hard, cleared my throat while mentally checking my short list of what it meant to be a man and attempted in the same thought to double-check the list with what my dad and life taught me. Five minutes later I was done. I had shared my top three keys to manhood, and I was rather pleased. The most profound things in life are simple, short, and reproducible.

My advice: keep the Great Commandment and the Great Commission. I told Judah to (1) love Jesus, (2) love the women that God has placed in his life (mom, sisters, aunts, grandmas, cousins, and a potential future wife), and (3) train his kids, grandkids, and, if the Lord allows, his great-grandkids to do the same. As he grows older, I will expand his vision to include disciple making outside of his family circles. He does not realize it but he is already seeing me model it for him, when he asks why I get up so early on Tuesdays and Thursdays to meet with men at the Cozy Table. For now I want to keep the power of focus. I want

Judah to make disciples, Lord willing, of my grandkids!

For the Christian, loving Jesus should be priority number one. Loving others should be the natural overflow of loving Jesus, but often disciple making as a practical application of loving others is over-looked.[22]

We do a lot of good things in the name of loving others. We faithfully serve in our church, share the Gospel with the lost, and go on mission trips, but are we making disciples? Frankly, disciple making is not convenient. Disciple making is hard. Disciple making takes time. Yet, can we afford to ignore disciple making because it is not convenient or because it is hard? Disciple making will be our legacy. In addition to our legacy, disciple making leads to maturity. In the next section we will take a closer look at how disciple making leads to maturity.

Disciple Making Leads to Maturity

Disciple making produces maturity in both the disciple maker and the disciple. While the disciple maker is stretched in his or her obedience, the desired outcome is always that the disciple matures and replicates.

The goal of the Christian life is maturity which glorifies God. Romans 8:28-29 states,

And we know that God causes all things to

*work together for good to those who love God, to those who are called according to His purpose. For those whom He foreknew, **He also predestined to become conformed to the image of His Son** [emphasis added], so that He would be the firstborn among many brethren;*

The apostle Paul picks up this train of thought in Romans 12:1-2,

*Therefore I urge you, brethren, by the mercies of God, to present your bodies a living and holy sacrifice, acceptable to God, which is your spiritual service of worship. And do not be conformed to this world, **but be transformed by the renewing of your mind, so that you may prove what the will of God is, that which is good and acceptable and perfect** [emphasis added].*

The goal of the Christian life is not to become a "good" Christian man or woman, a church attendee, or even a church member. The goal is to be conformed to God's will and transformed into the image of Jesus. But the Christian life does not end with self, nor are these life-giving changes an end to themselves. These changes are a means to an end. Maturity bears fruit in an individual Christian's life, but making disciples bears fruit in our own life (obedience and maturity) and the life of others (obedience, maturity, and replication). Obedience and maturity are great, but replication is even better because God's glory extends beyond your life into the lives of others.

We live in a highly individualist culture that conditions us to ask the question, "What is in it for me?" "If I am going to follow Jesus, what will I get from Jesus?" Subconsciously the answer to this question for many of us is often either (1) I will experience a blessed life or (2) I will grow in my maturity.[23] Yet, Jesus calls us to look past the fruit of our own life to be used to produce fruit in the life of others.

Could it be that we as Christians or the Church are asking the wrong questions? Are we focused too much on "What am I?" or "How do I get?" Have we forgotten the "why" of Christianity?

The "why" of Christianity is to become mature followers of Christ who reflect Christ and glorify Him.[24] As Christians we have been called to share the good news of the Gospel which is part of disciple making, but we have also been commanded in the Great Commission to make disciples, followers of Jesus who have a mature faith that glorifies God.

Simon Sinek in his best-selling book *Start with Why* (2009) challenges the status quo of the business world by questioning business corporations' practice of defining their goal or strategy for the company by using the questions "what?" or "how?"[25] Sinek argues that the business world should instead be asking "why?"

Sinek gives the example of Apple and the technology industry. Why has Apple for two decades consistently made superior products? They start with answering the question, "Why are we doing what we are doing?" In contrast Sinek argues that most companies neglect to even mention why they do what they do. Instead they just state "what" (the goal) and "how" (the strategy) they will do what they do.

Not Apple. Apple starts with "why." It is the core of their marketing and the driving force behind their business operations. To help illustrate this point, imagine if Apple also started backwards by creating a marketing message that started with "what" which might read, *"We make great computers. They're user friendly, beautifully designed, and easy to use. Want to buy one?"*

While these facts are true, I am not sold. We instead want to know *why* they are great and user friendly. Turns out Apple has figured this out over the years and knows better. Here is what a real marketing message from Apple might actually look like: *"With everything we do, we aim to challenge the status quo. We aim to think differently. Our products are user friendly, beautifully designed, and easy to use. We just happen to make great computers. Want to buy one?"*

See how different that feels? Because Apple starts with the "why" when defining their company, they are able to attract customers who share their fundamental beliefs. As Sinek puts it, "People don't

do. They buy *why* you do it." Starting
akes Apple more than just a computer
ng features, and that is why their
: flourished while their competitors'
products with similar technology and capabilities
have often flopped.

The same is true for us. If we ask "what do we do?"
The answer is we make Christians. They are good
people, saved saints, and fill our churches. Do you
want to be one? If we ask "how do we do what we
do?" We might say share the Gospel, give them a
Bible, and invite them to church. If we ask "why we
do what we do" the answer is we want to make
disciples of Jesus, mature disciples who replicate.
They are sinner-saints, striving to decrease so Christ
may increase, seeking to make disciples and glorify
Jesus in all they do. Do you want to join us?

Sinek does not have a Christian worldview, but he
may be on to something. There is application for us
as Christians. Do we understand the "why" of our
faith? Some common answers to the "why" of our
faith are:

(1) To gain Bible knowledge through Bible study,
    prayer groups, small groups, Sunday school class,
    and the sermon.

Bible knowledge is wonderful and necessary but has
this focus of feeding self-led us to become spiritually
lethargic as Christians. We come to church, get fed,
and nothing really happens beyond this. We sit on

the sidelines with a lot of head knowledge and love many things that are not "bad" but are not Jesus.

(2) To create church members.

I am all for membership. Let me be clear, if you love Jesus, you will love His bride! As we discussed earlier, church membership is vital. The church is a greenhouse where you and I can grow. In most churches, if you are not a member you are limited in the degree that you can engage. But perhaps a better argument for church membership would be: The church is the bride of Christ. Jesus loves the church. Why would you not want to be a member? Remember, if you love Jesus, you will love what He loves. You will even put up with other imperfect church members and their imperfect pastors. Yet, membership of a local church is not the "why" of Christianity.

(3) To share the Gospel and see people saved.

Evangelism is commanded (Mark 16:14-16 and Acts 1:8) and part of the "why" but it should not be the only piece of the pie when it comes to the mission of the Church. Evangelism produces new Christians, or put differently spiritual babies. The Great Commission is to make disciples who get the Great Commission and make disciples. Evangelism is part of disciple making, but there is more to disciple making than evangelism.[26]

Here you may disagree, so let me clarify. Evangelism

is the necessary first step to maturity in Christ. You must be "born" before you can become a "disciple" or a disciple maker. The Gospel is the foundation for all maturity in the believer's life, but maturity is developed over time and not in a moment. It would be nice if we could reach maturity quickly, but if we are honest we know that maturity is a product of time. Disciple making is not instantaneous; disciple making demands time. What is the tradeoff for time invested in disciple making, disciple making produces maturity in both the disciple maker and the disciple. This leads to another answer to the "why" of what we do as Christians that is good but not the ideal.

(4) To seek to produce maturity through good initiatives, such as Christian outreach, church attendance, or Christian programs. Again, these are good but do these activities produce disciple makers? If you believe that these initiatives do produce disciple makers, what are we asking people to replicate or make?

We cannot limit ourselves to focusing on our own maturity. If we do, we neglect Jesus command to make disciples. If we are walking with Jesus, we are to be coming along side others in order to "teach them to obey all I have commanded you." If we are not, the warning of Hebrews 5:12-14 applies,

> *"For though by this time you ought to be teachers, you have need again for someone to teach you the elementary principles of the oracles of God, and you have come to need*

milk and not solid food. For everyone who partakes only of milk is not accustomed to the word of righteousness, for he is an infant. But solid food is for the mature, who because of practice have their senses trained to discern good and evil."

Evangelism alone is not enough to produce maturity. I am afraid that much of our evangelistic efforts rely on leading a person to Christ and then trusting that God will grow a spiritual baby to maturity in the midst of a godless culture. While God is involved in our sanctification, it seems that He uses people in our lives to grow and mature us. We shake our heads when our newly saved neighbors and family members do not show up to church or continue to make poor life choices that hurt themselves and others. While these actions do not honor Jesus, why should a baby believer act differently? No one has taken the time to walk with and help the individual grow in greater maturity, no one has taken the time and energy to show what it means to follow Christ. No one has come along side to intentionally invest in them.

Church alone is not enough to produce maturity. Another scenario, which is slightly more optimistic, is when we lead a person to Christ and drop them on the steps of our church or introduce them to our pastor. The expectation is that if a new believer parks in the pew for an hour on Sunday each week they will become mature followers of Christ. Or if they are introduced to our pastor, that the pastor will be able to connect with them to help them in their journey to maturity. Yet, the reality is we are more relationally connected with our spiritual child than our pastor whose plate is relationally overflowing. Remember, your pastor's job is to equip you for the work of the ministry (Ephesians 4:10-12). Our job is to make disciples.

Christian programming alone is not enough to produce maturity. A final and even yet sadder scenario is taking place with our children and grandchildren. Spiritual maturity is not made by entrusting future generations to the church's youth group. Again, don't miss my heart in this example. Strong youth groups are a blessing from the Lord and can greatly complement a parent or grandparent's effort to nurture spiritual formation and maturity in their loved ones. Apart from knowing Christ, the friends that our children choose to invest in will have the greatest influence on their lives during their formative years. Youth group leaders can and should be powerful role models in the lives of students. A healthy youth group is an immeasurable blessing.

Yet the idealistic concept of a youth group is not a fail-safe plan for disciple making. As parents and grandparents, we are selling ourselves short if we believe that the youth group will ensure that our children and grandchildren catch Jesus. As a father of four the buck stops with me when it comes to my kids' spiritual maturity. Yes, my kids will make and be responsible for their own decisions as they approach adulthood, but I will do my best in the limited time I have to lead them to Christ and then disciple them. I want them to be life long disciple makers. Remember, the church and its programs are designed to be a greenhouse. Dads and moms make disciples. People make disciples.

People, not organizations or programs, make the best disciples. God has commanded you and I to make disciples. Our obedience to take the Great Commission seriously has the potential to produce maturity not only in our lives but will allow God to use us to produce maturity in the lives of others.

This leads to our last reason to make disciples. Disciple making brings purpose. You and I were born not just to mature, but also to reproduce; we have been commanded to replicate.

Disciple Making Brings Purpose

Jesus did not leave us as His followers without direction. We are called to move beyond conversion (a baby Christian), beyond being a disciple (a learner) to become disciple makers (a guide, a coach, a teacher). We are called to share the Gospel, invite others to church, and center our lives on the Bible, but there is more to Jesus' command to "make disciples." We are to replicate followers of Christ who take disciple making seriously.

Why? Because disciple making leads to eternal fruit.

Matthew 6:19-20 states,

Do not store up for yourselves treasures on earth, where moth and rust destroy, and where thieves break in and steal. But store up for yourselves treasures in heaven, where neither moth nor rust destroys, and where thieves do not break in or steal; for where your treasure is, there your heart will be also.

People find purpose in lots of things: careers, families, hobbies, entertainment, and a host of other pursuits. We transfer our love of these pursuits to others. If we love sports, we make athletes out of our children. We invest hundreds of hours, spend lots of money, and give lots of time training and coaching them. If we love the arts and value education, we send our kids to the best schools, try to expose our kids to different art mediums, give our kids private instrument lessons, and closely guide their every effort. If we love the outdoors or recreational pursuits then we take our kids on camping excursions, bike rides, or hunting trips and teach them, give them pointers, and train them to love the endeavor. If we love work and money, we train our kids to work hard, save, invest, and make wise financial decisions.

We replicate in others that which we love. While sports, the arts, recreation, and financial pursuits are all wonderful, the pursuit that God gives to us as followers of Christ is to love Jesus, love others, and replicate Jesus in the lives of others. We are to teach others to love Jesus and model for them how to teach others to love Jesus. We are to make disciples. As followers of Christ, why would we not find joy in helping to reproduce a love for Jesus in the life of others? After all, Jesus is to be our first love.

This chapter has offered five reasons for making disciples: disciple making (1) is commanded by Jesus, (2) is the Biblical Norm, (3) secures the next generation, (4) leads to maturity, and (5) brings purpose beyond self. This raises the question, why would we not make disciples? Chapter four will explore four reasons that Christians struggle to engage in disciple making.

CHAPTER 4
Why are We NOT Making Disciples?

While some are involved in making disciples, many
are not. Why? There are different reasons for the
lack of disciple making in our churches. The design
of this chapter is to define the challenges that many
churches are facing in regard to disciple making.
This chapter is also intended to encourage pastors and
church leaders to examine how they are investing
their ministry time and the leadership capital that they
have been given. I understand that there is a fine line
between a helpful critique and hurtful criticism. My
heart is not to discourage the Church and ministry
leaders but to encourage and equip each to grow in
disciple making.

In this chapter we will look at four broad reasons we
are NOT making disciples: our culture, the pew, the
program, and the pastor.

Disciple Making Struggles to Thrive in an Individualistic Culture

We live in a culture that leans toward narcissism and
consumerism, e.g. "all about me" and "more for me."
These cultural tendencies have not helped disciple

making. While there is a lot of talk of discipleship programming in our churches, discipleship is different from disciple making. Discipleship is about you and me. Discipleship doesn't drive replication. In contrast, disciple making is about someone else and drives replication. Unfortunately, some don't believe that disciple making applies to them. Instead they believe that it is the professional's job.

Disciple making seems to go against the very DNA of American independence and individualism. If you go back into our nation's humble beginnings you will find indentured servants. But even one of our founding fathers, Ben Franklin, did not like the idea of being an indentured servant to his brother for nine years. Frankly, disciple making, to the individualistic American mind, does not feel very American. We prefer the John Wayne approach of pulling up our bootstraps and following Jesus alone or maybe the more modern sentiment proclaimed by the boy band the Backstreet Boys who crooned, "I want it that way!"

There are exceptions. Mentoring is popular in some sectors of the business world, typically initiated by those who are interested in being developed. Mentoring in the context of the business world is ultimately an avenue to network, leverage self-promotion, and drive the success of the mission of the company. Yet, disciple making in a Christian context is unique. Disciple making's goal is to make much of Jesus versus climbing the corporate ladder.

One would hope that disciple making would be alive and well in our churches. Yet, if you can name the man or woman (not your pastor) who intentionally invested in your progress of becoming a disciple, you are probably unique. Many believers have never had a spiritual mentor. Instead many rely solely on the greenhouse of the church or their pastoral staff to assist them in maturing as a disciple. This is not ideal and falls short of what we find in Scripture.[27]

In short, the local church struggles to make disciples. As an entity the church was never designed to make disciples because you and I as individuals are called to make disciples. The pastor cannot be the only one to make disciples. Ask any pastor and he would tell you while he like Paul would like to be all things to all men, he cannot effectively make disciples of his entire flock. Many pastors cannot effectively shepherd more than 100 people and shepherding is a lot different than disciple making. This leads to the second broad reason we are not making disciples: the plight of the pew.

The Plight of the Pew

There are many reasons that Christians do not make disciples, but four stand out as the great obstacles for Christians to make disciples. These are busyness, confusion, an un-biblical view that disciple making is the pastor's job, and the lack of role models.

(1) Disciple Making Takes Time.

We can be too busy by choice. We all have twenty-four hours in a day; so did Jesus. We have families, careers, responsibilities, hobbies, and we go to church and all of these good things take time. If we compare day planners and Google calendars with our friends we may both agree that our lives are too full. But should we be too busy or our lives be too full to take Jesus' command to make disciples seriously? Are good things keeping us from great things?

Remember disciple making is not the same as discipleship. Both are important but they are fundamentally different. Discipleship relates to you. Disciple making is relating to someone else. Often, we have no problem engaging in church programs which help us grow, but we give little or no time for expending energy or a block of time to invest in another person.

When we hear discipleship we think of personal growth. Consider the terms we use interchangeably with discipleship. Terms such as *becoming more like Christ*, *spiritual growth*, *spiritual journey*, *spiritual maturation*, *sanctification*, or *spiritual formation*, are often used interchangeably with discipleship. Interestingly enough, all of these terms point to our own Christian development and not to the development of another.[28] Disciple making is something different. It is others-centered.

Deitrich Bonhoeffer, Christian author and martyr, stated, "Be aware of the guy who has a dream of community and is not in a community."[29] To put a twist on Bonhoeffer, be aware of the guy who has a dream of becoming Christ like but is not engaged in the lives of others making disciples. We are left to wonder if our shift toward individualism and self in the context of discipleship and disciple making is the effect of our individualistic, Western culture. Bonhoeffer would not be pleased, but more importantly neither would Jesus.[30] Jesus commands us to make disciples, but there seems to be a lot of confusion surrounding discipleship and disciple making.

Discipleship is not the only place we get turned around. Ed Stetzer writes,

> There is a confused understanding in the churches today between discipleship and disciple making. Discipleship can be reduced to a 6 week or semester long 'program' in church. That seldom works for disciple making. Disciple making cannot be reduced to a program. Disciple making requires life on life, i.e. spending time with people. Mark 3:14, *'And He appointed 12 that they should BE WITH HIM...'*
>
> Disciple making requires someone willing to give their time. Here we need another paradigm shift if we are going to see more biblical disciple making. We need to train people to be willing to invest time in people. Sadly, most believers are friendly, but they will not commit to giving their time. Many

people hoard their time for TV, entertainment, and the pursuit of materialism, rather than the development of disciple makers. We tend to be too absorbed in our own little orbit, and we like it that way. This value system has to change.[31]

If unwillingness to invest our time for disciple making wasn't enough to dampen our enthusiasm for disciple making, the misplaced expectations of disciple making being accomplished by the ministry professional totally extinguishes the disciple making flame.

This leads to the second obstacle found in the pew, confusion.

(2) Confusion.

Six years ago, I began serving as an adult education pastor in a medium sized church located in a rural area of the Midwest.[32] The church, almost fifty years old, had four generations of Bible-believing, Jesus-loving people. The church doors are open Sunday morning for two services and Sunday school, Sunday night service, and Wednesday night for prayer meeting. The church boasted Sunday school attendance of 90% of those who attended worship services – I checked and double-checked this number when I was hired because I thought it was an erroneous statistic. The church is intentionally evangelistic to the community and missional to the world. I consider myself blessed to be serving at a very healthy, evangelical church.

Six months into my tenure as education pastor, we began to offer growth groups (topical Bible studies) to add variety to our Wednesday night prayer meeting. We lined up our best teachers and launched this extra dose of biblical teaching, and roughly 100 adults of all ages attended. We were ecstatic! Roughly twenty percent of our church attendees voluntarily chose to be engaged in a six-week Bible study. By attending these Bible studies, they were being exposed to God's Word in church four times in a given week (Sunday service, Sunday school, Sunday night service, and a Bible study setting). As I had the cream of the crop at my fingertips and my title was education pastor, I decided to conduct a brief, eight-question survey to see where our people were on their spiritual journey.

This survey included questions such as: "On a scale of 1-5 how vibrant is your prayer life?" and "How many times a week on average do you read the Bible outside of church?" The last two of my eight questions were oriented toward disciple making:

- Are you engaged in disciple making?
- What is disciple making?

The responses were telling. While almost every participant answered my first six questions, only a few answered the last two questions. In answer to: "Are you engaged in disciple making?" most didn't feel that they were engaged in disciple making. In answer to, "What is disciple making?" I received only three attempts at a definition.

I was stunned! I had surveyed godly, Bible-believing people who were engaged in church. These were Christians who love Jesus. These were followers of Jesus who want to be obedient to Jesus' will for their lives. These were church members who are motivated to get into God's Word. They were giving four hours a week to church and Bible study![33] They were doing everything their pastors were asking them to do, yet were they engaged in disciple making? Survey says . . . they didn't think so, or at least they were unsure. This confusion, surrounding disciple making, leads to the third obstacle found impacting the pew, an incorrect view of the professional pastor.

(3) Disciple making is the professional's job, not mine.

Sadly, this is the sentiment of many in the pew. The pastor does the ministry and I, the church member, support him. Yet Ephesians 4:11-12 states the pastor's primary responsibility.

> *And He gave some as apostles, and some as prophets, and some as evangelists, and some as pastors and teachers,* **for the equipping of the saints** *[emphasis added] or the work of service, to the building up of the body of Christ.*

Did you catch it? The pastor's primary calling from

Scripture is to equip the saints. While all Christians, including pastors, have been commanded to make disciples (Matthew 28:19-20), pastors have specifically been tasked with the responsibilities to equip the saints to be able to make disciples. And, while not exempt from disciple making, they should not be burdened with the sole responsibility to make disciples.

Remember the comment by the father who was meeting with his son in the opening story. He stated that his own dad was a "godly Christian man," yet he failed to take time to intentionally invest in his son? His vocation? He was a pastor. He was too busy to give time to make disciples of his children.[34] It is easy to see how the unbiblical expectation placed on pastors to be "the professional disciple maker," has resulted in pastors doing "good things" in ministry while often neglecting the great things. Great things like the opportunity to invest in their own children to make disciples. This leads to our last and probably greatest obstacle of making disciples, the lack of role models.

(4) Lack of Role Models.

Of all the reasons for not making disciples, this may be the most prevailing. As the statistic from Barna reflects, disciple making is not being talked about enough nor is it being modeled effectively. Your church may be the exception to the rule and doing remarkably well in disciple making, but churches often place emphasis on discipleship and not disciple making.[35] By and large when people use the term "discipleship" they think of a program that will help them grow in their own faith. The Great Commission calls us not to personal growth but to replicate growth in others.

What makes disciple making so challenging? In his book, *Discipleship*, Robby Gallaty underscores that the problem lies with ignorance and uncertainty surrounding disciple making. Bob Smietana, in his article *Most Christians Want to Be Better Disciples. They Just Don't Know How to Get There,* quotes Gallaty recounting his own personal experience, "'I wandered aimlessly in my Christian life, uncertain of how to proceed . . . When people in the pew don't know what to do . . . they don't do anything at all.' That's left many churches struggling to fulfill one of the central tasks of the Christian life: making disciples."[36]

People need role models. Remember what Paul told the Philippians, "Join in following my example and observe those who walk according to the pattern you have in us" (Philippians 3:17). Many have never seen disciple making. Very few Christians ever see disciple making taking place so they struggle to know what disciple making looks like.

So why is my pastor not talking more about disciple making? Careful, he may be talking about disciple making. You and I just may be distracted by programming that results in in our own personal growth (discipleship) instead of the personal growth of another (disciple making). This moves us to our third broad reason we are not making disciples.

The False Hope that Programs will Make Disciple Makers

Church programming is not bad, in fact they can be very productive in helping to accomplish church goals. Programs are valuable and useful, but they are tools, not disciple makers. People, not programs, make disciples. The church can be compared to a greenhouse for the Christian. Every week Christians fill sanctuaries and Sunday school classrooms. Throughout the week church members participate in small groups to study the Bible. They engage in discipleship programs through men's, women's, youth, and children's ministries, invest countless man-hours and resources into fellowships, outreach opportunities, and equipping opportunities. Food pantries, recovery groups, and counseling programs look to address the physical, spiritual, and emotional needs of those connected to our churches. We have in-reach programs: greeters, first impression, welcome desk, and ushers. We have outreach programs: local evangelism, hospital visitation, and mission trips. We have committees, teams, choirs, soloists, instrumentalists, and orchestras. Some even have hand-bell choirs. Here are three observations concerning programs.

(1) Programs are good and have value, but they will not foster a disciple making mentality/environment.

A recent survey of LifeWay Research found that of 2,930 United States Protestant churchgoers, 19% read their Bible every day and another 26% read their Bible a few times a week.[37] John Wilke shares in his article, *Churchgoers Believe in Sharing Faith, Most Never Do*, that 61% of Protestant churchgoers have not shared their faith in the past six months, another 25% have shared 1-2 times in the last six months, and only 14% sharing 3 or more times in the past six months.[38]

Bible reading and evangelism are not the same thing as making disciples. But it would be difficult, if not impossible, to be a disciple of Jesus let alone a disciple maker if one were not consistently in God's Word and willing to evangelize. Though we rightly value and need our church programs, are they having the desired effect, i.e. resulting in life change of believers?[39]

(2) Programs are great for maintaining but not so good for multiplication.

Is it a fair question to ask, "What is the end goal of our Christian programming?" It might be to produce a pipeline of leaders: Sunday school teacher, church event coordinator, small group facilitator, greeter, usher, counselor, evangelist, a team member, a choir member, part of the band, a church planter, a missionary. But was this Jesus' goal for making disciples? Biblically we serve in these roles because Jesus gives spiritual gifts and calls us to be engaged in His body. Jesus has promised to build His church.

We are called to make disciples.

For the sake of acknowledgment, programming produced the pipeline of leaders mentioned above. Those that currently fill these leadership and service roles were not always engaged in these good works. In many cases these men and women are growing believers or even new believers who rightly want to serve. They are being followers of Jesus who are blessing others through the use of their spiritual giftedness and their faithful service. They are in a sense being "disciples." In its own way the church is creating disciples within these programs as these ranks are grown and replenished. One could even make the argument that at the changing of the guard there is a form of replication taking place, but again we must ask ourselves is our end goal to make disciples to serve in the ranks of our programming? Or is our goal to replicate spiritually mature believers who are able to replicate other spiritually mature believers? Are we investing in people for the sake of the kingdom or are we investing in positions for the sake of our programming?

This raises several questions. Have we drifted from our marching orders? Are we more concerned with building the church (filling leadership roles) than executing the Great Commission (creating followers)? The majority of our church programming is necessary for the church body to have structure as it gathers together to worship, but programs are a poor strategy for making disciples. Disciple making is program resistant.

Are our leadership strategies producing a generation of disciple makers or are they sustaining a church for a generation? The steep decline in evangelicalism and a mass exodus of Millennials from the church indicates that the answer is the latter. We tend to blame a spiritually darkening culture for our decline, but could it be that we as evangelical leaders have been casting a vision that has fallen short? Have we placed our hope on strategies that perpetuate programs instead of produce disciple makers? This leads to the next reason that we may not be majoring on disciple making.

(3) Programs are people-oriented, but they are not relational enough to make disciples.

Disciple making resists programming because disciple making demands intentional relationships that are designed to reproduce. I was reminded of this recently when Gary wandered into my office on a Sunday morning. As Gary walked through the door, I shot him a question at him. "Hey, Gary, how are you enjoying our time together?" A couple weeks back, I had invited Gary to meet with me and another man. We had connected once a week over the last four weeks for the purpose of reading through the book of John, memorizing scripture, praying, and talking about Jesus Gary grinned and said, "It's great, I really enjoy it." He continued, "You know I've been in church for over 25 years, and I've always attended Sunday school, but I've never done anything like this." I asked him what he meant. He paused and said, "My wife and I attend together, and we have had great, solid Sunday school teachers, but I'm the type of guy that won't speak up . . . I guess I hide. While I get a lot out of the lessons, I don't engage. But when we meet together, there is nowhere to hide and it pushes me to grow and become more like Jesus."

Programs, like Sunday School and small groups are a great thing and an important part of discipleship, but they take tremendous energy to sustain and often have a limited shelf life. Discipleship programs may be complex but disciple making is simple. Disciple making requires intentional relationships that are designed to reproduce. Disciple making is sustainable and transcends generations. Programs are good; disciple making is commanded. This leads to the last great challenge to disciple making, the challenge of the professional.

In the rest of the chapter I would like to take the opportunity to speak directly to pastors. As professional pastors we face many challenges when it comes to making disciples. We may give disciple making verbal affirmation and then fail to follow through with our own action plan. A wise preaching professor I had in seminary liked to state that he was "preaching beyond his own obedience." As I write, I am aware that the following ideals may be beyond my own obedience and as a fellow pastor I pray that God gives both you and me the humility and grace to not only preach but to obey immediately and with the right heart attitude the guidance of our Savior.

The Challenge of the Professional

Several years ago, while I was attending seminary in Dallas, Texas, my dad recounted a disheartening story in an effort to impress upon me the priority of disciple making. Dad had dropped by to see a friend of his who was a retired pastor. In the course of their conversation, my father asked his friend whom he could list from his ministry who had been discipled through his pastoral efforts of over three decades. Who had he invested in? The pastor dropped his head and in a moment of candid introspection stated that he had preached many sermons, shared the Gospel many times, led many meetings, counseled many people, and even built a church building, but there was no one that came to mind whom he felt he could say he had made a disciple. To be fair, this pastor may have been having an extremely bad day and have taken a pessimist view on his influence. I want to be sensitive here as pastors have unbelievable demands on their times. Ministry never stops. The pastor is required to wear more hats then most of his professional peers. Yet, it is important for us as pastors to consider how and where we invest our time. We must not let the tyranny of the urgent keep us from where Jesus has called us to follow.

Tommy Kiker in his excellent book, *Everyday Ministry*, helps put disciple making in context for a pastor. Dr. Kiker writes,

> I have already spent some time in exhorting a focus on intentional personal evangelism.

However, the Great Commission calls us to do more than JUST evangelize. A pastor has to be about the work of making disciples and equipping the saints for the work of the ministry. The pastor should spend some time in making disciples of the entirety of the congregation, and this is done in the context of large teaching moments. But the pastor should also have relationships where he is pouring into small groups and individuals . . .

If you are going to be an effective disciple-maker, you have to spend time with those you disciple. The ultimate goal is multiplication (much better than addition). Paul writes, "The things which you have heard from me in the presence of many witnesses, entrust these to faithful men who will be able to teach others also." (2 Timothy 2:2). The pastor ultimately should desire to produce disciples, develop leaders, and delegate ministry "for the equipping of the saints for the work of service" (Ephesians 4:12).[40]

There are three questions we should ask as pastors: (1) *What does Jesus mean by disciple making?* We must know our goal. (2) *Who am I intentionally investing in?* We must know our target *and* (3) *What am I reproducing?* We must know the outcome.

There are many reasons that as pastors we may struggle with disciple making, but four rise to the top:

(1) Pastors are too busy to make disciples.

Pastors remind me of those gifted individuals who can spin multiple plates at one time. While we look calm on the outside and seem to have all the right answers, we are really running around madly trying to keep ministry plates from dropping. Think of a duck swimming on the water. He looks calm above the water but below the surface he is paddling like crazy. If you are a pastor reading this book, you probably have zero margin and energy to take on anything else in an already full ministry schedule, let alone giving time to make disciples. Yet, we cannot afford to miss the opportunity to make disciple makers who will in turn make other disciple makers. We cannot afford to miss a kingdom investment that has the potential for multiplication beyond our scope. The individuals we invest in will be the future backbone of our church, its ministry efforts, and the next generation to carry the torch of our faith.

One of the things that I have appreciated about my own senior pastor is his encouragement for me to meet with men who are both older and younger. I am almost 40 years old and I have found myself meeting recently with 20 year olds, 30 year olds, and men in their sixties. My senior pastor understands that all of these men have the potential for tremendous influence in our church body.

(2) Pastors are overwhelmed by their role in disciple making.

As mentioned above, many pastors feel the responsibility to do every aspect of ministry. As pastors, we have a unique calling, e.g. "the equipping of the saints for the work of service." The most prevalent responsibilities of a pastor tend to be preaching, shepherding, and leading. Yet, as pastors we are also followers of Jesus and are therefore not exempt from the Great Commission. As a pastor, I am commanded to make disciples, too.

Not only are we as pastors called to make disciples, but also as leaders we need to help our people define disciple making. As previously suggested, the majority of individuals in our churches are doing discipleship, but very few seem to have a clear idea as to what disciple making is. As pastors, and therefore leaders, we must be willing to give a clear vision of disciple making to our people. The pew will not rise above the expectation set in the pulpit. As Howard Hendricks aptly stated, "A mist in the pulpit leads to a fog in the pews."[41] As pastors we must have a clear vision of disciple making to lead others in disciple making, which brings us to the third broad reason we are not making disciples.

(3) Pastors must rely on more than just preaching to facilitate disciple making.

While preaching is necessary for setting the standard proclaimed in Scripture and vision casting, disciple making requires more than just vision casting. Disciple making is caught not taught. Disciple making must be modeled. Here again, I am thankful to my senior pastor who is intentional to invest in lives of other men in the context of meeting with a few for the purpose of disciple making. Not only does he afford me the opportunities as his discipleship pastor to pursue disciple making, he also commissioned me to write this book and its companion small group lessons in order to provide our church with a clear vision for disciple making. Yet, of these three: modeling, empowering, and vision casting, his modeling of disciple making lends the most weight to the disciple making effort at our church.

You may ask, "Why won't preaching by itself make disciples?"

Pastors are called to preach; it is the high duty of their station. In fact, preaching is the number one thing that congregations look for in prospective pastors.[42] The call to preach is deeply rooted in Scripture beginning with the prophets in the Old Testament and continuing with the Apostles in the New Testament. Preaching is a practice found in the New Testament church. Acts 2:42 states:

> *They were continually devoting themselves to the apostles' teaching and to fellowship, to the breaking of bread and to prayer.*

Preaching is consistently upheld throughout the New Testament. Paul declares to his protégé Timothy,

Preach the word; be ready in season and out of season; reprove, rebuke, exhort, with great patience and instruction.

Preaching is consistently upheld through church history. Churches that take Hebrews 4:12 seriously will continue to proclaim the truths of the Bible.

For the word of God is living and active and sharper than any two-edged sword, and piercing as far as the division of soul and spirit, of both joints and marrow, and able to judge the thoughts and intentions of the heart.

But preaching alone will not make disciples makers. Preaching, a one-way, verbal communication, from an educational perspective, is a poor medium.[43] This is reflected in Dale's Cone of Learning.[44] Similarly, Bloom's taxonomy's lowest level of learning is remembering.[45]

We remember very little of what we hear because listening is so often passive. Those in the pew are the receivers. Many will not remember what was preached after their Sunday afternoon nap.

Should preaching be abandoned? Absolutely not![46] Preaching is the proclamation of God's Word and God's Word is effective. Paul admonishes the young pastor, "All Scripture is inspired by God and profitable for teaching, for reproof, for correction, for training in righteousness so that the man of God may be adequate, equipped for every good work" (2

Timothy 3:16, 17). Preaching is the great burden of the pastor. The proclamation of the Word is both a mystery and a joy.

Yet, preaching left to itself will not make disciples. We can see this in Jesus' ministry. Jesus preached, but the bread and butter of His disciple making efforts were the teaching opportunities within the context of quality time with His disciples. Disciple making is primarily learned by living life alongside another person. Disciple making is caught, not taught.

As pastors, we need to remember three things:

1. As a pastor, we have the greatest leadership capital.
2. As a pastor, we cannot lead others where we will not go ourselves.
3. As a pastor, if we do not have personal convictions regarding our engagement in disciple making, neither will our people. Remember, "A mist in the pulpit leads to a fog in the pew."

(4) Poor exegesis and faulty teaching can create confusion around disciple making.

The interpretation of the text of Matthew 28:18-20 has led to much confusion regarding disciple making. Many equate Matthew 28:18-20 (the Great Commission) to Romans 1:16, Acts 1:8, and a host of other passages involving evangelism. Yet, the command of Matthew 28:19-20 is to make disciples. While disciple making involves evangelism, there is more to disciple making than evangelism.

Evangelism is necessary and commanded for every believer, but evangelism is a part of the Great Commission not the whole of the Great Commission. This does not mean that we must pit evangelism against disciple making. This would be foolish and self-defeating. Evangelism is the necessary first step in making a disciple. And a healthy disciple maker of Jesus shares the Gospel. Disciple makers evangelize because evangelism is a necessary part of disciple making.

There is always the potential for faulty teaching in the church and seminary settings. If we take the Great Commission, Matthew 28:19-20 and taught (or implied) that it equals "sharing the Gospel," we have sold the Great Commission short. There needs to be a paradigm shift in thinking that evangelism is a necessary part of disciple making if we are ever going to see a surge in disciple making.

This line of thinking does not advocate that we abandon evangelism. On the contrary, it solidifies the necessary place of evangelism in disciple making. Disciple making and the proclamation of the Gospel are the responsibility of every believer. If not careful, the poor interpretation of Scripture and weak exegetical preaching will create a fog in the pew.

In the next chapter we will look at the "when" of disciple making.

<u>Consider:</u>

* In your own words what is disciple making? Or what do you believe are the necessary parts of disciple making?

Remember making a disciple is more than a Gospel presentation, giving someone a Bible, and a church invitation, all of which can be important. Evangelism is commanded in Acts 1:8, 2 Timothy 3:16-17 stresses the importance of the Bible, and fellowship with believers is commanded in Hebrews 10:24-25. But these activities left to themselves are not disciple making.

<u>Reflect:</u>

* Who intentionally invested in you to help you grow in your walk with Jesus or made you a disciple?

* Have you ever seen disciple making modeled?

* Are you making disciples?

Let's look at our definition of disciple making again.

> *Disciple making is an intentional spiritual investment in the life of another believer focused on modeling and teaching how to follow Jesus so that the other believer can replicate other believers who will follow, model, and teach others to follow Jesus.*

Apply:

- Do you need to ask someone to invest in you so you can learn to make disciples?

- Do you need to invest in someone else so that you are engaged in disciple making?

Pray:

Before moving to the next chapter, take a minute and talk to the Lord about making disciples. If the idea of making disciples scares you, tell the Lord and ask Him for courage. If you are excited at the thought of disciple making, tell the Lord and ask Him to give you opportunities to fulfill His command. Pray for a heart for disciple making; Jesus wants us to make disciples. In the next chapter we will explore when we will be ready to make disciples.

CHAPTER 5
When Will I Be Ready to Make Disciples?

A couple months back, we had a new intern at our church. As I processed with him the ministry opportunities in which I hoped he would be able to serve, I could sense his excitement. He would help facilitate in our grief share program, lead in our Helping Hands ministry, be part of outreach teams, teach his Sunday school class, shadow a professional counselor, attend our staff meeting, memorize scripture, beef up his prayer life, write out his testimony, and walk through a ministry book with me.

"Does this all sound good," I asked. "Great!" he responded. "One more thing," I said, "I want you to go find two other guys to meet with, walk alongside them through a book of the Bible, help them grow in their pursuit of Jesus, and teach them how to replicate." The intern's face fell. He was unsure. Now, he had been unsure when I mentioned public speaking, and had honestly expressed that he was terrified of public speaking, but he was willing to give public speaking a try. But when it came to investing in someone else, I thought he was going to throw in the towel. "I don't know if I can do that.

What makes me qualified to meet with other guys? I mean, you are a pastor so I understand why you are qualified but I am not."[47]

The intern was willing to be discipled, willing to engage in church programming which would make him square up with his greatest fear of public speaking, but he had the hardest time envisioning himself engaging in disciple making.

The Great Commission, to go make disciples, was originally given to ordinary men and women who believed in the person of Jesus and took His commandments seriously. If we consider the "eleven" disciples (Matt. 28:16), the majority were uneducated Jewish fishermen. These men were simple and probably a little rough around the edges. They lived in a day when there were no church buildings, no discipleship programs, no New Testament, just men and women who taught other men and women how to follow Jesus. By God's grace, Jesus' first disciples were very successful at making other disciples. Yet, Christians today are confused, scared, or possibly just plain disinterested in making disciples. Could God really use me to make a disciple?

Remember, people, not programs, make disciples. Disciple making is not serving, evangelism, or missions though these are to be hallmarks of the Christian life. Disciple making is not our personal devotional life, though our personal time with Jesus is imperative for the vitality of our faith. There are many good and useful things that should be a part of a Christian's life: personal time in the Word, prayer, scripture memory, and a steady diet of good preaching. We should also be engaged with other believers in Sunday school or small groups, Bible studies, and serving in the church. We should be committed to His Church and giving of our resources, time, and talents. Believers should be serving outside the church, committed to evangelism, and going on missions. These are godly activities, but they do not make us a disciple maker.

Paralleling discipleship activities and disciple making, David Kinnaman writing for the Barna Group states,

> Despite believing their church emphasizes spiritual growth, engagement with the practices associated with discipleship leave much to be desired. For example, only 20 percent of Christian adults are involved in some sort of discipleship activity—and this includes a wide range of activities such as attending Sunday school or fellowship group, meeting with a spiritual mentor, studying the Bible with a group, or reading and discussing a Christian book with a group.
>
> Practicing Christians are more likely to be involved in a variety of spiritual growth activities than are non-practicing Christians... Yet, even among practicing Christians, fewer than half are engaged in these four types of

spiritual development [The four groups are: (1) Sunday school or fellowship group, (2) meeting with a spiritual mentor, (3) studying the Bible with a group, or (4) reading and discussing a Christian book with a group.] Only 17 percent say they meet with a spiritual mentor as part of their discipleship efforts.[48]

According to Kinnaman, only 17 percent of practicing Christians find themselves in a disciple making context. Yet, when it comes to disciple making, interns are not the only ones who wonder if they can be used. As pastors, we often struggle to lead effectively in disciple making. We often don't feel qualified to come down out of the pulpit or outside of the neat lines of our programming and get behind a cup of coffee with the intent to pursue Jesus in a setting that perhaps demands more transparency than we are used to. Just because someone is a pastor doesn't mean that they don't struggle with insecurities when it comes to disciple making. Kinnaman writes,

> Christian adults believe their churches are doing well when it comes to discipleship: 52 percent of those who have attended church in the past six months say their church "definitely does a good job helping people grow spiritually" and another 40 percent say it "probably" does so. Additionally, two-thirds of Christians who have attended church in the past six months and consider spiritual growth important say their church places "a lot" of

emphasis on spiritual growth (67%); another 27 percent say their church gives "some" emphasis.

Church leaders, conversely, tend to believe the opposite is true. Only 1 percent says, "today's churches are doing very well at discipling new and young believers." A sizable majority—6 in 10—feels that churches are discipling "not too well" (60%). Looking at their own church, only 8 percent say they are doing "very well" and 56 percent "somewhat well" at discipling new and young believers. Thus, pastors give their own church higher marks than churches overall, but few believe churches—their own or in general—are excelling in discipleship.[49]

Remember what I stated previously, organizations do not make disciples; people make disciples and if people are going to make disciples their leaders must cast the vision. It is not that complex.

So when will you and I make disciples? The following are three hurdles that we must cross before we will begin to make disciples. Let's look at the first hurdle, fear.

Hurdle #1: Fear - *I must be willing to allow faith to triumph over fear.*

The entirety of this book up to this point has been designed to stir within you and I the need to engage in disciple making. Consider the following question,

"What do you think is the number
one reason people fail to make disciples?"

1. Disciple making is the church's job (the organization not me, the individual).
2. Disciple making is the professional's responsibility (the pastor).
3. Disciple making is a spiritual gift, and I don't have it!
4. Programs make the best disciple makers.
5. Evangelism is disciple making.
6. Discipleship is disciple making.
7. I am not commanded to make disciples.
8. I am afraid of making disciples.
9. I do not know where to start making disciples.

What is your greatest hang up regarding disciple making? If you answer was number 8 or number 9, then the rest of this book is for you!

I often tell my kids when they worry about a job I've assigned to them, "Kramers do hard things! You can do it! I wouldn't have asked if I didn't think you could do it!"

Jesus has asked us to make disciples. Disciple making is a hard ask! Christians can do hard things or Jesus wouldn't have asked. We know that faith triumphs over fear. Not because our faith is so strong, but because the object of our faith is able and worthy!

Ephesians 3:20 reminds us,

Now to Him who is able to do far more abundantly beyond all that we ask or think, according to the power that works within us to Him be the glory in the church and in Christ Jesus to all generations forever and ever. Amen.

Jesus' promise at the conclusion of the Great Commission is designed to comfort and steel our hearts. Never forget Jesus' promise in Matthew 28:20,

> *And I will be with you even to the end of the age!*

Don't miss that the context of this precious promise is going and making disciples. Remember, fear of the unknown is not failure, and failure in the past is neither fatal nor final. Fear that leads to paralysis to do the right thing, to be obedient, to make disciples is the mortal enemy of faith. Let's move to the second hurdle of disciple making which is closely related to fear. It is the hurdle of not feeling qualified.

Hurdle #2: Qualified - *I must trust that I am immensely qualified.*

You and I are qualified to make disciples if we are following Jesus. There are no perfect followers. Yet, despite our imperfections God can use us. In Matthew 4:19, Jesus makes a bold statement to His disciples. "Come follow me and I will make you fishers of men." There are many who claim to follow Jesus, but in actuality they are following other things. If you place other things above Jesus, you will not make disciples. You may make disciples of your other pursuits, but you will not make disciples of Jesus.

You are qualified to make a disciple even if you are not a Sunday School teacher, a small group facilitator, or a leader in your church. Disciple making is not just for leaders; it is for all followers of Christ. Being a Sunday School teacher, small group facilitator, or a respected leader does not mean that you are a disciple maker. Disciple making transcends spiritual gifts, status, talents, and personality. Disciple making looks more like being a coach, mentor, or an along-sider.[50]

Our pasts often give us pause when it comes to disciple making. How could I teach someone else when my past and even my present is marked by failure?

2 Corinthians 5:17 and Galatians 2:20 answer this logical question. Both of these verses state that we have new identities in Christ. On this side of the cross our identity is to be found in Christ. One of Paul's favorite phrases in the New Testament is "in Christ." He mentions "in Christ" and other like phrases 216 times in the New Testament. Paul had a dark past, but a very present Savior. Paul made disciples.

Peter denied Christ and in the Gospels he is enthusiastic, strong-willed, impulsive, and, at times, brash. Peter was flawed, but Peter influenced John Mark (who was not a disciple of Jesus). John Mark wrote the Gospel of Mark, which recounts Peter's story of Jesus. Peter experienced failure, but Jesus restored Him. Peter made disciples.

Disciple making may feel like a stretch, but it is not unattainable. Remember, Jesus promised right after He commanded us to make disciples that He would be "with us." Let's look at a third hurdle that we must cross in order to make disciples.

Hurdle #3: Commitment – *I must be willing to try to make disciples.*

All great spiritual work begins with prayer. Prayer is where we align ourselves with God's will, access His power, and see His presence in our lives and circumstances. When we don't know where to turn in the face of an overwhelming challenge or impossible circumstance, prayer should always be our first impulse.

   (1) Start with Prayer

Prayer is the gateway to disciple making. I have been blessed to attend and serve in solid, Bible-believing, God honoring churches. These churches have ranged from a small non-denominational church consisting of several families to a flagship Southern Baptist mega-church.

As a youth, I attended a Lutheran grade school where I participated in a year of eighth grade confirmation classes and as a college student, I attended a Presbyterian church that paid for a good percentage of my theological education. Throughout my ecclesiastical (church) journey I have attended churches in big cities, college towns, and rural, small town America. The good news is that, for the most part, these churches are led by and filled with godly people whose hearts desire to follow Jesus and glorify God. The bad news is that I was never approached by anyone in my journey who offered to invest in me in order to develop my relationship with Christ from merely being a 'convert' to becoming a disciple maker.

Do not misunderstand me: discipleship was talked about. I heard a lot of sermons and spent hours in Sunday school, and even more time in small group settings, but within the context of the church, no one discussed with me my need to become a disciple maker. It was assumed that I would know how to read my Bible, how to pray, and how to engage in the other spiritual disciplines. It was assumed that I would actively share my faith, give of my possessions, and serve both inside and outside of the four walls of the church. It was assumed that if the pastor preached it, I did it! It was assumed that disciple making (replication) was taking place.

I was fortunate, my parents loved Jesus and intentionally discipled me. My parents also modeled what being a disciple maker looks like as they selflessly invested time in the lives of others. When I went to college, I decided that I needed to buckle down and grow in my faith, in a sense now that I had moved out of my parents' house I needed to own my faith for myself. So, I joined a para-church ministry on campus and went directly to the leader and asked if he would disciple me. After asking multiple times over a month, he met with me for a year after which he moved his young family to Lebanon to become missionaries. After this experience, I began to pray that I too would have the opportunity to make disciples.

I did not just want to be invested in. I wanted to invest in others. I asked God to make Matthew 4:19 (fisher of men) and the Matthew 28:19-20 a reality in my life. As I studied my Bible, other verses began to make it into my prayer life like 2 Timothy 2:2. Prayer is always the gateway into disciple making. The Lord likes answering prayers that are consistent with His will, such as "Lord, make me a disciple maker . . ."

Once we are willing to pray, we must be willing to make space on our calendar. We must intentionally make time for disciple making.

(2) Make Time for Disciple Making

We are busy! We have families, careers, responsibilities, hobbies, and besides we go to church and all of these things take time. Compare day planners and Google calendars with any of your friends and you will both agree that your life is too full. But should we be too busy to take Jesus' command to make disciples seriously?

The adage that we worship our work, work at our play, and play at our worship, is perhaps too close to the reality of our situation. As followers we are to be different, and one difference should be how we prioritize our time. Many of us believe that we are doing disciple making because we are involved in discipleship activities. But what are we "making," replicating, or reproducing spiritually in the lives of others around us?

Remember disciple making is not the same as discipleship. Both are important but they are fundamentally different. Discipleship relates to you. Disciple making is relating to someone else. We have no problem engaging in discipleship but often find little or no time for expending energy or a block of time to invest in another individual's life.

It seems that we have traded discipleship or disciple making for more personal or possibly self-serving terms such as *becoming more like Christ*, *spiritual growth*, *spiritual journey*, *spiritual maturation*, *sanctification*, or *spiritual formation*. Interestingly enough, all of these terms point to our own Christian development and not to the development of another. Once we have cleared our calendar, we must take action.

(3) Be Intentional to Act in Obedience

Organizations struggle to make disciples. The church as an organization does a great job encouraging and equipping the saints, but people make disciples. Pastors are not the only people called to make disciples. Let the "professionals" do their job (specifically, helping support and equip you, the saint). Will you and I be obedient and do the work of the ministry? Will we make disciples?

Christ commands His followers in the Great Commission to make disciples. You may feel that you are already doing lots of great things for Jesus. You might think, "Is it ok if I just focus on these good things and let others (perhaps more qualified people) make disciples?"

Scripture is clear on the answer to this question. He wants you and I, His followers, **to make disciples**. Jesus wants obedience. In fact, Jesus' love language is obedience. John 14:21 states,

> *He who has My commandments and keeps*
> *them is the one who loves Me; and he who*
> *loves Me will be loved by My Father, and I*
> *will love him and will disclose Myself to him.*

It is important that we understand Jesus' love language. We do not get to choose Jesus' love language. I am reminded of an exercise that I often apply in pre-marital counseling. After discussing Gary Chapman's insightful book, *The Five Love Languages*, which offers five different ways that people like to show love and be shown love, I ask the very nervous groom-to-be if he can identify the preferred love language of his bride-to-be. Most of the time, the young man smiles confidently and selects from the list of five love languages (20% odds of success) what he believes to be his future wife's love language. He quickly becomes bewildered when she shakes her head no and nervously laughs.

I had been married about two years when, one day while my wife was away at work, I decided to impress my wife and deep clean our entire apartment. Two hours later, after breaking a sweat, I stood back and assessed my cleaning prowess. I had managed to hygienically clean our two-bedroom apartment to where I would have been comfortable to eat off of any surface in the house. I had reorganized our closets and even cleaned the pesky baseboard lip that collected dust. Ah, true love!

I waited for my wife to get home like an excited puppy, anxious for his master's return. As my wife came through the door, she dropped her purse on the recently cleared and Lysoled counter and declared that she was exhausted. She then proceeded to the straightened couch and plopped down on it kicking her shoes off into the middle of the newly swept floor. I waited . . . and waited . . . and then said, "Did you notice I cleaned the whole apartment?" Instead of jumping off of the couch, squealing in delight, and planting a nice big kiss on me, she sank deeper into the couch, opened one eye, and then mumbled, "Thanks. Boy I'm tired!"

I have since learned (you might say painfully) that acts of service are not my wife's love language. She likes them, but she does not love them. Instead she loves personal notes, the mushier the better. Surprisingly, I stink at writing love notes. I'm a horrible speller and I despise my handwriting. Yet, I want to love my wife so I need to learn to speak her love language. It does not really matter what I would prefer to do. In the same way, we may be doing a lot of good things for Jesus, but are we being obedient to the Great Commission? Are we speaking Jesus' love language?

Christ commands us to make disciples. Most of us have never tried disciple making before and probably already think we would stink at disciple making. Yet, Christ's love language is obedience. Jesus is the biggest fan of us learning to make disciples. Like anything, disciple making is a process.

We want to love Jesus. When we obey Him, we show we love Him. Will you pray that God would allow you to make disciples? Will you carve out time to invest in another individual? Don't worry, God will provide the grace. He likes to use us in our weaknesses; this is where He is most glorified. He always provides the grace for His calling. Never forget the last part of the Great Commission. It is a promise to those who become disciple makers.

> *Go therefore and make disciples of all the nations, baptizing them in the name of the Father and the Son and the Holy Spirit,*

*teaching them to observe all that I commanded you; and lo, **I am with you always** [emphasis added], even to the end of the age.*

So when will you and I be ready to make disciples? We will be ready to make disciples when we in obedience tell Jesus "yes" we are willing to try to make disciples. The journey begins and continues with prayer. Tell the Lord you are ready to make disciples. Remember, Jesus is with you! In the next chapter we will look at where we can begin our journey as a disciple maker.

CHAPTER 6
Where Can I Begin to Make Disciples?

Perhaps the greatest challenge to making disciples is knowing where to begin. Many have never had the example of another individual investing in their lives and the thought of disciple making is a great unknown. In this chapter we will look at the simplicity of disciple making, specifically (1) where we can look to make disciples, (2) what character qualities makes a good disciple, and (3) where we can find disciples who will make disciples.

Fortunately, Jesus speaks directly to the question of where we should look to make disciples in the Great Commission. Let us look closer at His instructions. In Matthew 28:19 Jesus instructs His disciples,

> ***Go*** [emphasis added] *therefore and make disciples of all the nations, baptizing them in the name of the Father and the Son and the Holy Spirit.*

Our English translation of the original New Testament text in Matthew 28:19 has led to an incorrect application of the verse. We have placed the emphasis of Matthew 28:19-20 on the first of the three participles, "Go." "Go," "baptizing," and "teaching" in the Greek are all participles.[51] Yet in the Greek the weight of this verse lies primarily on the imperative verb, "Make disciples." Another rendering in the Greek for "Go" is "as you are going make disciples."

I hear the word "go" and I feel tired and on some days overwhelmed. I feel I'm back in high school lined up at the starting line for a cross-country race. I am already busy and I don't want to go. But if you tell me "as you are going . . .", this somehow feels a lot better. Let me give you an analogy. My wife may say to me, "Michael I forgot to buy bread and I was planning on making peanut butter and jelly sandwiches for lunch, will you go get me a loaf of bread at Save-a-Lot?" This means that my plan to mow the yard before lunch or my latest woodworking project has now been put on hold until I go to the store. One more thing has been added to my already full checklist. But if I tell my wife, "I am going to the gas station to get gasoline for the lawn mower so that I can mow the yard." And she says, "While you are going, can you pick me up some bread?" Suddenly, buying a loaf of bread seems much easier to accomplish.

We read, "Go therefore" in our Bibles and then believe we have to pull up our tent pegs and become missionaries. While some may be called to be missionaries in a foreign land, the majority of us are not called to relocate overseas to make disciples. We are called to make disciple makers right where God has planted us.

We read, "Go therefore" and believe that we have to sell our home, quit our job, and relocate across state lines to attend Bible school or seminary to become a pastor. While you may be called to full-time ministry, equipping and shepherding the saints, the majority are not called to be pastors. Most are called to be businessmen, coal miners, farmers, teachers, doctors, homemakers, engineers, and construction workers.

Sometimes we read, "Go therefore" and think that this doesn't apply to us because we actively attend, give, serve, or teach in our local church. We feel that we are already vested in the Great Commission. But the call is to make disciples and the placement of the participle "Go" at the beginning of the sentence shares the weight of the command that follows it, "make disciples."[52]

So where can we make disciples?

In Community

In his book, *Making Room for Life: Trading Chaotic Lifestyles for Connected Relationships*, author Randy Frazee introduces the concept of life circles. The concept of life circles is easy to understand and a very practical tool that can be applied to disciple making. Frazee states, "Life circles are relationships with people who are nearby – where community can take place."[53] Our life circles are our "As you are going." Let me give you an example of my life circles. I live in a rural town of 6,000 people in a county of 40,000 people in the rural context of southern Illinois. My life circles are as follows:

1. Home circle: my immediate family & my extended family.
2. Work circle: my co-workers and the waitresses at the local diner where I meet with other men.
3. Worship circle: my church family and my Sunday school class.
4. Extracurricular circle: the gym in West Frankfort where my daughter takes gymnastics.
5. Sports circle: the basketball and soccer leagues where my kids play sports.
6. Neighbor circle: my neighbors, the neighborhood kids that play with my kids.
7. Other friends' circle: friends from out of state.
8. Social media circle: while I am not on Facebook, I am a teaching assistant for an on-line class and I post videos once a month on my church's website.

Your life circles will be different than mine. Take my wife for instance. Her life circles are as follows:

1. Home circle: her immediate family and extended family.
2. School circle: other moms that she has

connected with.

3. Exercise circle: ladies that she leads in group fitness.
4. Library circle: ladies she has met at our public library.
5. Worship circle: her church family and Sunday school class.
6. Neighbor circle: connections she has made in our neighborhood.
7. Other friends circle: friends from our time in Texas and Georgia.
8. Social media circle: my wife has about 1,000 Facebook friends.

If we are going to make disciples, they are going to come from our life circles. For most, their greatest influence will be in their Jerusalem where they are in relationship with others. Others will have unique platforms that allow their life circles to reach beyond their Jerusalem. Jobs, education, and the ability to travel freely allow the ability to influence outside of our local communities. Some will even have the unique privilege of time, health, and resources to travel around the world. For those who are not able to travel, social media has made our ability to "connect" almost limitless.[54]

Jesus was a carpenter; His job didn't require travel. Jesus never boarded an airplane; they didn't exist. He didn't have radio, television, or Facebook account. It is informative to reflect on the fact that Jesus never left a one-hundred mile radius in the course of His ministry life. Yet, Jesus was the ultimate disciple maker. Jesus didn't let His circumstances dictate His impact on others. Perhaps we need to make disciples like Jesus? Maybe His way was most effective.

Every Tuesday at 6 a.m., a group of six guys meet at our local diner, the Cozy Table. They are all baby-boomers. Three are retired, one owns an auto body shop, one runs a construction outfit, and the other works for the highway department. Why are they there? Because one man, who likes to fish, decided to go fish for men (Matthew 4:19). He invited two other men to read the Bible. A couple weeks later, two other men were invited to join the group. What are they doing besides eating breakfast? They are working their way through the Gospel of John, spending time in prayer, memorizing Scripture, and encouraging each other to become more like Christ.

God has planted these men in the same life circle, at our church. If you ask any of them how this group is working out, they would tell you it is a great thing because they are growing in Christ more and faster than they have for a long time. It all happened because one man (who happens to love to fish) invites two other men from his life circle to go deeper with Jesus.

We can make disciple making too complex. Because of this we avoid engaging in making disciples. We may engage in ministry or serve at our local church, but we fail to make time ("as we are going") to walk intentionally alongside someone to teach him or her how to love and follow Jesus. We fritter away our lives doing good things but fail to do a great thing like leaving a spiritual legacy. Where should we start in making disciples? Disciple making starts by simply asking someone to meet with you for the purpose of pursuing Jesus together.

A couple weeks after wrapping up walking through the book of John with two men who happen to be brothers, I was meeting with one of the men to check up on him and he commented, "Did you know that my brother is meeting with two guys and reading through the book of John?" "No," I responded, "How did he do it?" He shrugged his shoulders and said simply, "He asked them."

Disciple making starts when one individual decides to invest in another and is willing to take the initiative to invite them to pursue Jesus together. Yet, it is not enough to ask just anyone. It is important whom you invest in. You and I are busy and our time is limited. While Jesus loves everyone, it is important that we invest in those who will bring good return. We need to invest in faithful, available, and teachable men and women; F.A.T. people.

The Right People Are Everything

Jim Collins in his book, *Good to Great*, stresses the importance of surrounding yourself with the right people. Collins calls it, "Having the right people on the bus."[55] This principle is nowhere truer than with disciple making. Investing in the wrong person will make for a doomed and miserable disciple making experience. As I have already alluded to, you must be a follower of Jesus in order to be or become a disciple maker. Those who are not willing to be a disciple will never make disciples.[56]

As a pastor, I will give time to anyone who expresses interest in studying the Bible or learning more about Jesus. Taking five weeks to read through a Gospel, like the book of John, is a good investment. If the individual is lost, you can introduce them to Jesus and His claims in the Bible. If the individual who expresses interest in studying the Bible is a young believer, you can model the spiritual disciplines and provide accountability to help the individual grow in their pursuit of Christ. But even the lost or those that want to grow can be mediocre investments when it comes to disciple making.

The lost may meet with you because they are lonely, social butterflies, or think that meeting with you somehow makes them a "good" or "better" person. Even those who know Jesus, may meet with you for the same reasons as the seeker who does not know Jesus. Believers also may meet with you just to learn more about the Bible or Jesus. They may be interested in their own personal growth, but not be willing to replicate themselves in others. These individuals are often better served in a Sunday school, small group, or organized Bible study.

The church is designed to be a greenhouse for the believer, but you and I are called to carry out the Great Commission, to make disciples who will make disciples. Your relational capacity and time to invest in disciple making is precious. We must maximize our relational investments for the sake of the Kingdom.

Two observations I have made over the last two decades concerning the people who make good disciple making investments. First, we want to invest in people that are willing and committed to engage with the church. Going to church does not make you a disciple of Jesus or a disciple maker, but it is the best place for you to grow, be encouraged, be equipped, and be challenged to engage with fellow believers in a redemptive way.

Church is the biblical place to use your spiritual gifts, as already mentioned. The church is also an excellent pond to fish for potential disciple makers. The church is a greenhouse that is designed to nurture the believer's faith. The church is a family that is designed to be together in community. There is power in numbers whether 50 or 5,000. Be aware of the fallacy of those that say they value community, but are not living in community.[57] While there is no perfect church, pastor, or fellowship, Jesus loves His bride; we should love the Church too. Disciple makers love the Church.

I had the opportunity to lead a young man to Christ. He was a really likeable guy, easy to talk to, and very friendly. He worked a hard job, had a family, and enjoyed frog gigging in his free time. As soon as he said "amen" after accepting Christ, I began talking to him about reading through the book of John and memorizing Scripture. He gladly accepted my invitation to meet with him, and the next week we sat down over a cup of coffee at his kitchen table. Over the next five weeks, he came to church once. He left before the end of the service to get to work. We continued to meet and he continued to sporadically attend church. In contrast to his wife and kids never missed church. Yes, he had work, but our church offers four opportunities to worship each week. He was simply not willing to make the effort to get into the greenhouse.

There were other indicators that should have made me wary of investing extended extra time in this baby believer. I could not get him to memorize Scripture, his prep for our Bible study was sporadic, and he had vices that he would openly talk about but not release. He was open and honest about his struggles, but he was unwilling to allow Jesus to begin to work in his life. After three months, I began to realize that he would meet with me anytime but would not show up to church unless I continually pushed him.

While it is not bad to challenge a disciple to pursue Jesus harder, you cannot pursue Jesus for them. You should not have to push a disciple to follow. He must have the desire to follow Jesus. In the end, my friend's church attendance was non-existent, his vices began to reap their natural consequences, and he becomes a liability to those around him. Instead of being on a life-giving journey of making a disciple, I found myself caught in a reactive, life-taking relationship. I was my friend's lifeline instead of his coach or cheerleader.

Disciple makers are not designed to be a greenhouse. The church is the believer's greenhouse. Disciple makers are designed to be a stake planted in the ground next to a sapling by which the sapling can grow straight and true in the greenhouse. Church engagement is a great litmus test for aiding the disciple maker in making decisions as to who would be a good investment.

Secondly, we want to invest in people who are F.A.T. Those who are the best disciples and disciple maker material are individuals who are faithful, available, and teachable. They must be all three of these characteristics; if not, they will be flaky instead of F.A.T.

Those that you invest in should (1) be faithful to rise to the bar that you set for them in your time together, (2) be available to consistently meet, and (3) be teachable in the ways that God leads them to grow as they study the Word and pursue Jesus.

Faithful

Often we set the bar too low for those that we like and want to see succeed. Ultimately, we are afraid that they will fail and we don't want to set up our friends for failure. Yet, this misguided kindness often undermines the disciple making process. The goal is to call this individual to join you in making other disciples. Remember disciple making is not easy. Men and women who will eventually make disciples must be faithful to pursue Jesus. The goal of disciple making is quality not quantity, and quality is produced by faithfulness over time.

Available

If you seek to make disciples, many may accept your invitation to be invested in, but most will not make your investment a high enough priority to clear their calendar to be available.

On my last mission trip to Africa, I met a man named Michael who had recently come to faith in Jesus and taken his call to make disciples seriously. I heard of Michael when his mentor, Jimmy the head of thriving evangelistic ministry in East Africa, commented that he no longer invests in anyone who comes to Christ, but now looks to exclusively invest in "serious" men. While he is willing to share the Gospel with anyone, he would only invest in a select few. Jimmy then shared how Michael, "a serious man," had changed his strategy about disciple making and evangelism. Michael, like many others, had accepted Christ and shown great evangelical zeal to share with his family, friends, and neighbors. I asked what made Michael different. Jimmy shared that Michael woke up at 4 a.m. to walk on foot for four hours to meet with his team in order to be trained to make disciples. I left the conversation wondering, what would I give to become a disciple maker and what will God do with a man who is willing to get up at 4 a.m. and walk four hours over the African plain. East Africa should be put on notice; a disciple maker is being forged! What will you and I sacrifice to follow and lead other men and women to follow Jesus?

Like the rich young ruler, many genuinely want to follow but they will not make being a disciple a priority. They are too busy or too distracted chasing other things in life. They "like" Jesus, but they do not love Jesus. We make time for that which we love. We make time for that which is a priority.

It is crucial that we invest in individuals who make their pursuit of Jesus their top priority. Here we must pause and lend a little more clarity. There are those who may want to meet with you, but their current life circumstances will simply not allow them to be available. Do not fret; be wise, if there is a heart for Jesus there will be other seasons to invest and God will provide a way for that individual to become a disciple maker. If God through their circumstances has not allowed the time to be available, trust that God at the right time can clear their schedule. Disciple making is a process that is born out of repetition and time. Disciple making is caught not taught. Disciple making requires availability; it requires time.

Teachable

If you are not teachable, you cannot be a disciple and you will not be a disciple maker. A lack of teachability is a symptom of pride. The Scripture is clear, God is opposed to the proud but gives grace to the humble (Psalm 138:6, James 4:6).

I met with a man for six months. He was faithful, available, and I thought he was teachable. As we spent time together, this young man was faithful to read his Bible and our time was enjoyable. By all appearances he was teachable. He worked through his testimony, memorized Scripture, and was learning to pray. I was excited at his potential. The longer we met the more he began to share about his life. There were lots of things vying for his attention. How could I encourage him to follow Jesus? Our hour and half each week was not enough to prepare him to follow Jesus in a complex world. I began to encourage him to become more consistent with his engagement in church. He had a wife and kids that would gladly attend with him, but more often than not their extracurricular activities would compete with his commitment to be in church.

Week after week, having not seen him in church the Sunday before, I would try to encourage him to engage in a meaningful way with our church community. I explained that church was like a greenhouse for his faith and that a small investment on Sunday morning would propel his growth and bless his family. Once and a while he would attend, but more often than not there was an excuse for his absence.

As we continued to meet, I realized that this young man was simply not willing to shift his priorities from sleep, entertainment, sports, and family trips to engage consistently in church. He was teachable to a point, but he clearly valued other pursuits more than pursuing Jesus and was not willing to be teachable in this one area. He had come to a crossroads in his faith and was not willing to move forward in the one area vital to the growth of his faith.

After nine months of investing in this young man, we agreed to take a break. I communicated I'd be glad to invest again when his life was not quite as full. He agreed that it would be good to take a break. We enjoyed each other's company, but I think we both breathed a sigh of relief. He knew where he needed to grow and he no longer needed my gentle reminder. More importantly, I knew that where it mattered, he was not teachable.

Proverbs 13:18 and 18:2 state,

> *Poverty and shame will come to him who neglects discipline, But he who regards reproof will be honored.*

> *A fool does not delight in understanding, But only in revealing his own mind.*

Invest in the teachable. They are a good investment. Avoid nice men and women who are not willing to be teachable. They will not be disciple makers.

Where do we find F.A.T. people?

1. Your physical family - If you have young

children, you don't need to look further than your own home for your nearest and dearest disciple making candidates. Scripture is clear that disciple making begins at home. Deuteronomy 6 paints a wonderful picture of this ideal. The book of Proverbs also speaks to the transmission of truth within the context of the home: father to son as well as mother to children (Proverbs 31). Ephesians 6 continues the ideal of disciple making taking place in the home and lays the responsibility of disciple making directly on the shoulders of the father.

In our culture, many kids are growing up in a divorced home or a single parent scenario; God's grace will be sufficient in these circumstances. God is capable of using others to compliment a single parent's efforts. My own father grew up in a single parent household; he intentionally invested in me and is still investing in men around him. God is faithful!

2. Your spiritual family – While not all who profess Christ will follow Christ; intentional effort should be given to help those who God affords you the privilege to lead to Christ. As their spiritual parent, you are the most logical option to ground them in their newfound faith. Parentless, spiritual children are never the ideal.

3. Your church family – Church is a great place

to go fishing for individuals to invest in. But be selective. You don't want the contented or the curious. You want the committed!

I had the privilege of having an intern at the end of 2017. Robby is thirty years old, has a manly, foot-long beard, and more importantly loves Jesus. When I met Robby he knew he wanted to go to seminary as God was calling him to the pastorate. Robby was a unique investment. Part of Robby's internship was to walk through the book of John with me during our time together. As we met, I told Robby that the goal of our meeting together was not just so he and I would get to know each other, though this would necessarily happen. Our time together was not merely to come to know Jesus better, though we prayed this would happen. The goal was that Robby would make disciples who make disciples who love and serve King Jesus.

Shortly before Robby moved his family across state lines to attend seminary, I met with Robby for a cup of coffee. As I drove to meet with Robby, I wondered how I should encourage him. As I drove to our place of meeting, the Lord brought to mind the greatest regret that I had during my own seminary experience.

As we wrapped up breakfast, I encouraged Robby again to be a man who makes disciple makers. I then shared that when I was a full-time seminary student, I had moved across state lines away from family, was really busy studying, and I was not intentional to make disciples. Do not get me wrong, my wife and I were engaged in ministry.   Together, we worked eighty hours a month as urban missionaries seeking to have opportunities to share the Gospel with our apartment neighbors. We were in church every Sunday. I was an intern at our church and I co-taught a Sunday school class which required that every Saturday night after dinner I would spend seven to eight hours prepping to teach. I was surrounded by people. I was active in ministry. Yet, as I look back on this season of my life, I can name only one man that I intentionally invested in as a disciple maker. During the busiest and potentially most fruitful ministry season of my life, I did not make disciples.

Where do we make disciples?

We make disciples as we are going in our lives. This requires that we look up and see those that God has planted in our life circles. We look for Faithful, Available, and Teachable men and women.   We take the initiative to invite others to follow Jesus with us.

Disciple making is done where you are. Are you making disciples? Who are two people that are hungry to grow in their faith that you could invest in? Are you intentionally investing time in your kids or your grandkids to teach them how to follow Jesus? Where are you making disciples?

In our last two chapters, we will look at the "how" of disciple making.

CHAPTER 7
How Can I Make Disciples?

We have now examined the who, what, why, when, where of disciple making and we now turn to the *how* of disciple making. *How* is where the proverbial rubber meets the road for disciple making. Before we embark down the road of how to make a disciple, we would be wise to remind ourselves that disciple making resists programming. This means that any attempt to define one pathway for disciple making must be tempered by the realization that disciple making takes on different forms in different contexts. Yet, the DNA (a highly relational, spiritual investment in the life of another) and the outcome (replication of Christ followers) of disciple making remains the same.

Fortunately, Jesus doesn't leave His disciples clueless on how to make disciples. Not only did Jesus model disciple making, He reminds His disciples of the specific details of disciple making in the Great Commission, Matthew 28:19-20:

> ***Go*** *therefore and make disciples of all the nations,* ***baptizing*** *them in the name of the*

*Father and the Son and the Holy Spirit,
teaching them to observe all that I
commanded you; and lo, I am with you
always, even to the end of the age.*

Making disciples requires an intentional effort (go),
does not ignore the priority of the local church and
adherence to doctrine (baptizing), and calls for the
follower of Christ to impart what it means to follow
Jesus (teaching). While going, baptizing, and
teaching are clearly stated parts of disciple making,
implicit in disciple making is replication. Don't miss
the object of what is to be imparted through the acts
of teaching others. We are to teach others "to observe
all that I [Jesus] commanded." What has Jesus
commanded? His command includes the Great
Commission. We can't just teach people to follow
Jesus. We must teach people to lead others to follow
Jesus. Otherwise we haven't taught all that Jesus
commanded us.

Many may be tempted to apply the going and
baptizing pieces of the Great Commission while
neglecting to apply the "teaching them to obey all I
have commanded you" piece of the Great
Commission. The Great Commission seeks to foster
something greater than church programs,
humanitarian endeavors, and evangelical mission trips
can achieve. The Great Commission was not a call to
only replicate ministry leaders to serve as leaders in a
myriad of church programming. We are not called to
only replicate pastors and missionaries; these are
unique callings from God.

The Great Commission calls everyday followers of Christ to look beyond their pastors and missionaries to bear the burden of disciple making. Disciple making transcends a special calling, our spiritual gift, or an appointed role within the church. The Great Commission is for every believer who is seeking to faithfully follow Jesus. Where do we begin? How do we make disciples? Let's look at the first part of our definition for disciple making.

> <u>Disciple making is an intentional spiritual investment in the life of another believer</u> focused on modeling and teaching how to follow Jesus so that the other believer can replicate other believers who will teach others to follow Jesus.

An Intentional Spiritual Investment in the Life of Another Believer . . .

Sunday morning, my alarm went off at 5:30 a.m. As I got dressed, I mentally walked through what my responsibilities in church would be for that morning. Then I went and awakened my eight-year-old daughter. "Sophia, get ready. We are going to the Cozy Table." Thirty minutes later we were sitting in a booth with pancakes steaming in front of us. The next hour would be the highlight my day!

As we sat, we talked life. I asked her what is the hardest thing she faces in her life? She thought about it and responded, "Sometimes I am sassy." I responded, "Yep, that's a big one. Jesus will help you grow there. So will daddy and mommy. I love you, Sweetheart!"

After taking another sip of my coffee, I asked, "Critter, what do you think it looks like to follow Jesus well." She sat quietly and then shrugged her shoulders. "Sophia, let me give you four things. First, you need to love Jesus more than anything. Second, you need to love the people that God puts into your life like Jesus loves them. This will be hard, Sweetie, because people can be difficult. Third, you need to teach others how to love Jesus and others. And fourth, you need to find your beauty in the eyes of Jesus not in the eyes of some boy or even your daddy. Jesus thinks you are beautiful. He makes you beautiful."

I paused and asked if she understood. She nodded her head. Can you repeat these to me? Her young mind had no trouble listing off my four ideals for following Jesus well.

On the half-mile drive to church, Sophia piped up from the backseat. "Daddy, I struggle loving Jesus first! I love you the most!" "Sweetheart," I responded, "that's ok, the longer you walk with Jesus the more you will come to know Him and the more you will come to love Him. If you are obedient, your love for Jesus will grow. Jesus promises in John 14:21,

> *He who has my commandments and keeps*
> *them, he it is who loves me and he who loves*

me will be loved by my Father and I will
disclose myself to him.

"Do you understand?" I asked. She nodded her head with a satisfied nod. "Sophia, I think John 14:21 would be a good verse to memorize." "Me too, Daddy," she said.

I would do a lot of ministry that day, but perhaps the sweetest had just taken place. Disciple making begins at home! I have been blessed with four children, two of which have a personal relationship with Jesus. As a parent, I take them to church, provide for them, love their mother, attend their sporting events, buy them ice-cream, and a litany of other tasks, events, programs, and fun things. These are great things! But when I go to the Cozy Table, talk about Jesus, and help my daughter understand how she can be a better follower of Jesus, this is an outstanding thing! Yet it is not enough that I just teach her how to follow Jesus, my goal is that she can help others follow Jesus. I am shaping a future disciple maker, a fisher of women who I pray will spend her life reproducing other Christ followers. I want to take disciple making seriously. This means that I will intentionally spiritually invest in my kids. I want them to walk with Jesus, but more than just walking with Jesus, I want them to teach their kids, their grandkids, and others to live for Jesus. My kids are my disciples but I want them to become disciple makers!

Disciple making can take place at church, but if we

are honest this investment is limited in its impact by both the amount of time invested and the degree of commitment that individuals who attend church give to disciple making. We must be willing to self-critique and ask ourselves how much disciple making takes place on a Sunday morning in a one or two-hour time block consisting predominately of one-way communication platforms such as preaching and teaching.

Consider the following. The average person watches 3 hours of TV per day, spends 40 minutes a day grooming, and invests 1-2 hours a week in church attendance. Don't misread these statistics! Our church life is critical to our Christian walk. The church is the greenhouse of the Christian faith where we can be shepherded, encouraged, disciplined, and take part in programs that promote spiritual formation which help us grow and mature. The church is a place where we align our doctrine with the community under Scripture, practice the ordinances of baptism and communion, and exercise our spiritual gifts. The church is invaluable, but the church as an organization is not commissioned with making disciples that reproduce. People not organizations make disciples that replicate!

Many who fill the pews have little commitment or engagement past listening, serving, and social engagement. Again, listening to the proclamation of the Word, serving, and community are invaluable to the life of the believer. Preaching, teaching, and the community are powerful forces designed to influence semester or even a year or two. The ultimate goal is not to form a Bible study, but to become more like Jesus and to reproduce disciple makers.[58]

My free time on my calendar is currently limited by professional and familial obligations, but Tuesday, Thursday, and Sunday mornings at 6 a.m. I have discretionary time. These disciple making groups (D-groups) meet at the Cozy Table, with a purpose beyond fellowship. We commit to spend at least four times a week in the Word and to memorize two Bible verses each week. During our time together we pray, review verses, and discuss what God is teaching us in His Word. Each week we take turns sharing our testimonies, we memorize verses like the Roman's Road that gives us specific tools to be able to share the Gospel, and something amazing happens. As we get comfortable with each other we begin to open up and talk about our lives, our struggles, our victories, and where we need to grow in our walk with Jesus. We become, better husbands, better fathers, better friends, and stronger Christ followers. We become more committed to prayer, more committed to engage with the church, more committed to evangelism, and more consistent followers of Jesus. Ultimately, we become more like Jesus, but the goal is not that we become a more sanctified trio. The goal is that after a season together each of us identifies two other men to invest in. Disciple making was never designed to be a holy huddle; disciple making was designed to be a movement that impacts generations for Christ.

I am doing everything I can to make disciples. While

my "profession" is the pastorate, 6 a.m. breakfast meetings are rarely conducted during my work hours – work hours are filled with other ministry. Breakfast meetings at the Cozy Table with two other men is my plan for me to make disciples who make disciples. When I find a better plan or a better way to make disciples, I will adjust. The goal is to replicate disciple makers.

I have a disciple making plan. Do you? Your disciple making plan doesn't have to be the same as mine, but does your plan have the right DNA? Is your plan effective? Is your plan intentional? Is your plan producing disciple makers who are making disciples? Jesus said, "Go make disciples!"

Focused on Modeling and Teaching How to Follow Jesus . . .

We have seen how disciple making is intentional. We will now examine the middle part of our definition that comes from Jesus' command to make disciples through teaching.

> Disciple making is an intentional spiritual investment in the life of another believer focused on modeling and teaching how to follow Jesus so that the other believer can replicate other believers who will teach others to follow Jesus.

A Clear Goal – The DNA of Disciple Making

You will not make disciple makers unless you communicate your goal. Disciple makers make much of Jesus and intentionally invest in disciples who will replicate. Let's look closer at the DNA of disciple making.

(1) Make much of Jesus – The Great Commandment (Love Jesus, Love Others)

Disciple making is all about Jesus. We are not trying to make disciples that are like us. We are making disciples who become more and more like Jesus. Over the last two years, I have been attracted to John the Baptist's example in the book of John. John was a phenomenal leader who attracted people. John had disciples. John was a disciple maker who attracted men to God's message. Then Jesus came on the scene. John's response to his followers' concerns over John's disciples leaving John to follow Jesus is telling. John's words show the extent of John's humility. John simply tells his followers, "He must increase, but I must decrease" (John 3:30).

Disciple making is not about us. It is not about us looking good because we are keeping the Great Commission. It is not about us being the teacher, coach, mentor, or facilitator. Disciple making is about becoming like Jesus and pointing others to Jesus and that those we are pointing to Jesus point even more people toward Jesus. As you and I fall deeper in love with Jesus and better understand our

Savior's love for us, the only proper response is to pray for our sinful self and selfish desires to decrease and be made whole, beautiful, and complete which happens by Christ's increase in our lives. We should live to know Christ and make Him known.

How do we become like Jesus? How do we fall deeper in love with Jesus? We practice and teach what Jesus modeled. We dwell on the Word for there we find Jesus and God's will for our lives. We major in prayer for there we find the face of God. We memorize Scripture as Jesus modeled for encouragement, protection from temptation, conviction of sin, ability to share the Gospel, and the strength and courage to live this life. We engage in fellowship with other believers who can sharpen our walks with Jesus. We equip ourselves to share our faith with the lost. We share the Gospel with a lost and dying world. We find our identity in Christ and we engage in spiritual disciplines that will make us more like Christ. How do we do this in a disciple making context?

The following are five components that will help us in modeling Jesus. These spiritual disciples will help a disciple maker make much of Jesus.

1. Teach people to pray.

Disciple making is God's work and we need to be asking Him for opportunities. I make a habit of consistently praying with those I meet with, that God would provide them with individuals who will become disciple makers. We pray that Jesus would increase and that we would decrease (John 3:30). We pray for besetting sins and circumstantial struggles. I will ask those that I meet with to pray aloud with me. I encourage them to pray privately. I challenge them to pray big. Sometimes I even get to teach people how to pray. It does not get much better than hearing a babe in Christ say: "Dear God, this is so and so . . .."

E.M. Bounds wrote:

> Prayer cannot be retired as a secondary force in this world. To do so is to retire God from the movement. It is to make God secondary. The prayer ministry is an all-engaging force. It must be so to be a force at all. The estimate and place of prayer is the estimate and place of God. To give prayer the secondary place is to make God secondary in life's affairs. To substitute other forces for prayer retires God and materializes the whole movement.[59]

2. Stress the necessity of being in God's Word.

Fifteen minutes a day will change your life. I challenge those that I meet with to spend 4-5 times a week in the Word at 15-minute increments or longer. If they are already getting 4-5 times a week in the Bible, I challenge them to self-assess. Would it be profitable for them to get more time in the Word? They will always find they need more time. Scripture has an interesting property. Intake of the Word breeds a greater hunger for the Word. Spending time in Scripture is the number one indicator of spiritual growth in the life of a Christian.[60]

It is good to remember that people have different learning styles, be sensitive to this. Not all will take in the Bible like you do. Also, remember that the Bible is the hardest book ever written to understand. It is not a manual or a novel. It is the very Word of God and necessarily deeper than we can imagine. Spurgeon well stated, "Will God in very deed give us understanding? This is a miracle of grace. It will, however, never be wrought upon us till we know our need of it…let you man by faith cry, 'Give me understanding.'"[61]

I sat across the table from Richard and asked how his previous journey through John had been. He grinned shyly at me, "It was good, but I never read the assigned Bible reading before I came to the meetings." I chuckled and told him that I appreciated his honesty. "Why not," I asked?

"I have never been a good reader. I struggled to read in high-school and still to this day cannot focus. I'm not dumb as I can tear apart a car, build anything, and if you show me once how to track an animal or tie a lure I will never forget it; I'm just not a reader. When I listen to you teach in Sunday school, I can remember your points and recite the stories and illustrations that you use, I just struggle to read."

Again, I thanked him for his openness and then made a suggestion. "Richard, I think you are an auditory learner. You may not be a strong reader, but you compensate by learning with your ear. The next time you go deer hunting, pop in your ear buds and listen to a couple chapters of John on your smart phone. Let me know when you get through the book of John."

A couple weeks later, I received an exuberant text. "I did it! And I understood it! I got all the way through the book of John!" Richard is now in a small group Bible study and he is growing like a weed.

Richard is not the only one that I have had this conversation with. There are many highly intelligent men and women who struggle to get into the Word. It may be that they need to listen to it. Give them the freedom and do whatever it takes to set them loose in God's Word. They will grow and thank you for teaching them how to unlock the Word.

3. Memorize Scripture.

One of my favorite pastors, Chuck Swindoll, makes the bold statement, "I know of no other single practice in the Christian life more rewarding, practically speaking, than memorizing Scripture. That's right. No other discipline is more useful and rewarding than this. No other single exercise pays greater dividends! Your prayer life will be strengthened. Your attitudes and outlooks will begin to change. Your faith will be solidified."[62] I could not agree more. Scripture memory is by far the hardest spiritual discipline for most, yet an expansive knowledge of the Word at your fingertips makes you a formative tool in God's Hand for the glory of the Kingdom.

I meet with a prison guard named Derek and retired school teacher named Rod. I meet with them because they push me as a pastor and they are F.A.T. or faithful, available, and teachable men. Every Monday I know that I have to have my verses nailed down. Derek is competitive and loves the challenge of memorizing scripture. Coach, as we call Rod, while not as competitive, has a mind like a steal trap. Derek will hunt me down in the hall and push me to meet with him so that I will hold him accountable to memorize Scripture. Derek lived life fast and hard and then he ran into Jesus and turned 180 degrees. His co-workers knew the old Derek and are not quite sure what to do with the new Derek. At every opportunity, they challenge his actions and his faith. They ask him tough questions and point out his flaws, but when their lives blow up, they come to Derek looking for answers. They are watching him. Derek's response is to memorize Scripture so that he can give a defense of his faith. Recently he memorized 1 Peter 3:15 which states,

> *But sanctify Christ as Lord in your hearts,*
> *always being ready to make a defense to*
> *everyone who asks you to give an account for*

*the hope that is in you, yet with gentleness and
reverence;*

As Derek shared why he memorized this verse, I had
to smile. Here sits a state champion wrestler, who
runs in the heat of the summer, is known for being the
skull thumper of the cell block, turned Jesus lover,
who memorizes Scripture to give a gentle defense of
his faith. Derek is the real deal, a true disciple. Two
weeks ago, he led a young man, who is the new skull
thumper on the cellblock to Christ. He is praying that
God gives him the opportunity to meet with him and
another. Derek is a disciple maker.

4. Fellowship in the local church.

The book of Hebrews admonishes the believer in
chapter 10,

> *And let us consider how to stimulate one
> another to love and good deeds, not forsaking
> our own assembling together, as is the habit
> of some, but encouraging one another; and all
> the more as you see the day drawing near
> (Heb. 10:24-25).*

Jesus loves the Church. He died for her (Eph.
5:25), He is beautifying her, and He will
return for her. Those that love Jesus will love
what He loves.

Every believer has been given a spiritual gift.
Scripture is clear that spiritual gifts are

designed to edify the body (Eph. 4:12). There are many gifts and talents you can use to serve Jesus outside of church, but if you are going to use your spiritual gift in the way that Scripture prescribes you must engage with the church.

5. Evangelize.

The "good news" of the Gospel is that a sinner can accept a Savior who died, was buried, rose again, and will return. Romans 1:16 states the power of God for salvation is the Gospel. Evangelism is sharing the Gospel and the necessary first step of every disciple. But evangelism is not discipleship. Evangelism is not disciple making. But evangelism is a key component of disciple making. A disciple of Jesus is to share the Gospel (Acts 1:8).

Many struggle to share their faith. Both fear and the lack of preparation render many Christians powerless to communicate their faith. As a disciple maker, make disciples who can share the Gospel.

    (1) Teach them how to share their testimony – have them write in one page or less (1) what life was like before Christ, (2) what they believed when they came to Christ, and (3) what life looks like after coming to Christ.

Memorize

(2) Have them memorize salvation verses such as the Romans Road (3:23, 6:23, 5:8, 10:9-10, 10:13), Ephesians 2:8-9, John 3:16, Titus 3:5.

(3) Lastly: take those you invest in with you to share the Gospel. Take them to your neighbors. Take them to the senior adult center. Take them to a hospital. Take them on a missions trip. Take them, show them, and have them share their faith. Let them see you share your faith and then give them opportunity to share their faith.

While I have had many opportunities to take individuals overseas as part of mission trips where we train volunteers and then share our faith in an overseas context, I find the hardest place to share the gospel is within your own community. To do this often takes greater intentionality.

One evening last summer, I was scheduled to go out for Vacation Bible School follow-ups. Every year VBS follow-ups are a wonderful opportunity to connect with parents and also often leads to opportunities to share the gospel. This particular night, I invited Gary to join me. Gary and I had been meeting together and Gary had faithfully worked through and written out his testimony as well as memorized several gospel verses. Gary agreed to join me, but was visibly nervous, so I took point. Halfway through our visits we found ourselves standing in the living room talking with a single dad who had sent all three of his kids to VBS. While inquisitive, this man did not have a personal relationship with Jesus and was very interested in what we had to share. He intently listened as I began to share the gospel. He was attracted to the idea of Jesus, but didn't quite get his need for a Savior. As I paused in the conversation trying to evaluate if I was clearly communicating and whether the Spirit was working in this man's heart, Gary, though nervous, seized the initiative and began to share his own testimony how Jesus had worked in his life and saved him from his sin and a life lived for self. I'd love to say that this father of three accepted Jesus as his Savior that evening, but I am still praying that God would move in His life to a point of salvation.

Yet, Gary that night overcame his fear and clearly shared the gospel. He had a plan, took the initiative, and in the moment was bold to proclaim Jesus. I couldn't have been prouder, and Gary couldn't have been more excited. But none of this would have happened if Gary hadn't prepared and if I hadn't asked Gary to join me. By the way, Gary is now training to be part of an overseas mission trip to the slums of Africa to proclaim Christ in areas where Jesus' name has never been heard. We are to be faithful to share the gospel, and the Spirit will accomplish His purposes in the lives of others.

If the goal of disciple making is to make much of Jesus, then the key to disciple making is replication.

(2) The Key is Replication

The litmus test of disciple making is replication.[63] We do many great things under the banner of the Great Commission but if we are not replicating then we have missed Christ's intention. For instance, you may be involved in discipleship activities, but if these activities begin and end with your spiritual growth you are not replicating.

The goal of the church is to foster maturity in the lives of the believer who can then be a witness to a dark and dying world. The church's end goal is not to just make converts nor is it to just create discipleship opportunities. The goal of the church should be to make disciple makers who share the gospel, participate in personal growth opportunities, and replicate.

Here I would like to offer a word to pastors, ministry leaders, and people of influence within the church. Often, leadership within a church unintentionally looks to programming to create disciple makers. Yet, this will not work! People not programs make disciples. Programs attract people, but not necessarily disciple makers. As leaders we must be careful to resist the human tendency to count numbers, nickels, and noses lest we begin to believe that we are the ones who build the church.[64] Jesus will build His Church. As leaders we should have strategies and programs while praying that God would see fit to bless these endeavors, but as leaders we must be willing to be ruthlessly honest in (

critique of our programming. Is our programming producing disciple makers who are able to replicate?

Most pastors are stuck in program centric churches. If we do not like the results of our programming efforts, what can we do to begin to change unhealthy (or non-fruit bearing) church cultures? Before we answer this, let's consider the solo pastor or senior pastor. If this is your current calling, you may feel that your typical week finds you trapped by the demands of the pulpit or tied up by the boardroom. What can be done?

The answer is the same for both scenarios. You and I must choose to model disciple making. By modeling disciple making we will point our people past evangelism, beyond discipleship, to the goal of replication. The irony is as we make disciples they will propel discipleship and be the most proactive to evangelize. For most leaders, shifting the weight of their focus from programming, preaching, and pushing to disciple making feels foolish or at best seems inverse of what we think we should be doing.[65] Yet, isn't this how Jesus works, through our weaknesses and through His wisdom.

As leaders, we want to create a movement that goes beyond our influence and lasts beyond our lifetime. Good leaders lead; great leaders leave legacies. If we lead reactively instead of proactively our legacies will be greatly diminished. Leaders who are content with tyranny of the moment will miss the opportunity to launch movements.

So whether you are senior pastor, ministry leader, or a Sunday morning attender, how can you and I begin to leave a lasting legacy? Let's unpack the last part of our definition for disciple making.

So that the other believer can replicate other believers who will follow, model, and teach others to follow Jesus.

The following are three helpful principles, which will help a disciple maker to be more successful in disciple making. First, we must invest in F.A.T. people.

1. F.A.T

Remember, you want to invest in people who are F.A.T. Those who are the best disciples and disciple maker material are individuals who are faithful, available, and teachable. They must be all three of these characteristics; if not, they will be flaky (instead of F.A.T.)

Those that you invest in should (1) be faithful to rise to the bar that you set for them in your time together, (2) be available to consistently meet, and (3) be teachable in the ways that God leads them to grow as they study the Word and pursue Jesus.

Once we realize that we must invest in F.A.T. people, we are ready to grasp the reality that two are better than one.

2. Two are Better Than One

Ecclesiastes states that, "A chord of three strands is not easily broken" (Ecclesiastes 4:12).

Disciple making is more productive in a group of three than in a pair. There are always exceptions to the rule, but wisdom dictates that meeting with two others is more profitable than meeting with only one person. I encourage people to meet in groups of three in their disciple making endeavors for several reasons.

First, meeting in groups of three levels the playing field. I have found from experience that when you meet with one other individual there is an automatic and unavoidable distinction between the disciple maker and the disciple. I have had men sit down to meet with me who apologize profusely for not memorizing a Bible verse. They then justify their lack of discipline in light of my position as the leader of the group. Comments like, "Well, this is easy for you." or "I'm just the student and you are the teacher." are not life giving to the disciple making endeavor.

If we are honest, we live in a culture, which is not very comfortable with the concept of power distance (all are equals in a democracy) or disciple making.[66] I find that a group of three cuts through this weird dynamic and allows the disciple maker to take on the role of a facilitator, guide, or coach. Instead of the group requiring a leader, the group leads itself.

Meeting with two is also a better return on your investment. As our time is valuable and energy is limited. Why would we not meet in a group of three?

Now, I know there are exceptions. There are times when I would encourage the move to meet in a group of four, but these are rare. When might you consider doing this? Perhaps when the relationships or dynamics of the personalities being considered demand a group of four. Jesus had three men in His inner circle. James and John were brothers and Peter had a rather strong personality. Jesus was the disciple maker so this parallel is already unique unto itself. I have found from my experience that when you have a group of four, individuals can either become wallflowers or all can become frustrated because they do not get to talk enough.

There are times when one on one is preferred as well, but the longer I engage in disciple making the more convinced I am that disciple making is maximized in groups of three. It is important to be a good steward for the sake of the Kingdom.

Secondly, groups of three raise the bar on accountability. Even if you meet in groups of three, there may be a tendency for individuals to fall short of their commitments to read the Bible and memorize Scripture as they believe that the individual who has initiated the disciple making effort is so far ahead of them. This is solved by choosing to meet with two individuals who are relatively on the same page in their walk with Jesus. After one or two meetings, these two men or women will self-assess that they are on the same level and have been paired to run together after Jesus.

While a disciple may not rise to the expectation of the disciple maker, they will rarely fail to keep up their end of the bargain with a peer. In contrast to having people use me as an excuse for not memorizing a verse, I have watched time and again, one man nail a memory verse or complete his Bible reading only to hear the other man promise emphatically that he will have his verse or Bible reading pinned down the next week. That is positive peer pressure and it is priceless!

Thirdly, groups of three enrich the dynamic of the disciple-making group because personalities do not compete or weaken the group. For instance, in a group of two, if one individual is talkative and the other is quiet; one will always talk and the other will always listen. This is not ideal as a free flow discussion is preferred. In the reverse in a group of two talkative people, both may leave frustrated because they were continually trying to talk over each other or not given enough time to talk. How does adding another individual to this mix help? It helps by softening or tempering personalities. If one personality is dominant, two will better temper it. If one personality is reserved, two will do a better job drawing the individual out.

The challenge is that you are looking for two people instead of one. Again this is a blessing. You will pray harder and be more creative, neither of which will ever produce negative results. Three is a number that holds many advantages for disciple making.

Not only should we invest in F.A.T. people while maximizing our impact by realizing that two disciples are better than one disciple, but we should also continually remember the goal of disciple making, fruit. Disciple making is hard. Disciple making does not produce quick fruit, but it produces lasting fruit that can reproduce.

3. The Goal is Spiritual Fruit

Romans 8:28-30 states the goal of the Christian life,

> *And we know that God causes all things to work together for good to those who love God, to those who are called according to His purpose. For those whom He foreknew, He also predestined to become conformed to the image of His Son, so that He would be the firstborn among many brethren; and these whom He predestined, He also called; and these whom He called, He also justified; and these whom He justified, He also glorified.*

The goal of the Christian life is to be conformed to the image of Christ. In a word, we are destined for maturity which brings glory to God.

John 15:4-8 clearly depicts Jesus' heart for our lives,

> *'n Me, and I in you. As the branch*
> *bear fruit of itself unless it abides in*
> *so neither can you unless you abide*
> *in Me. I am the vine, you are the branches; he*
> *who abides in Me and I in him, he bears much*
> *fruit, for apart from Me you can do nothing.*
> *If anyone does not abide in Me, he is thrown*
> *away as a branch and dries up; and they*
> *gather them, and cast them into the fire and*
> *they are burned. If you abide in Me, and My*
> *words abide in you, ask whatever you wish,*
> *and it will be done for you. My Father is*
> *glorified by this, that you bear much fruit, and*
> *so prove to be My disciples.*

Christ's heart is that we bear fruit which glorifies God and proves that we are His followers. In John 14:12-14, Jesus gives His followers (you and me) an amazing promise,

> *Truly, truly, I say to you, he who believes in*
> *Me, the works that I do, he will do also; and*
> *greater works than these he will do; because I*
> *go to the Father. Whatever you ask in My*
> *name, that will I do, so that the Father may be*
> *glorified in the Son. If you ask Me anything in*
> *My name, I will do it.*

Can you imagine doing "the works" of Jesus? Can you imagine doing "greater works" than Jesus? Feels blasphemous, but that is what Jesus promises. Could it be that Jesus' last command to make disciples, to start movements that would impact generations, to leave behind a Christ follower who leaves a legacy is what Jesus had in mind? I think Jesus' disciples thought so. I think men and women who have changed their families, their generation, and begun worldwide movements in the name of Christ thought so. Are we limiting how God would use us? Is our vision too small?

Again Jesus' last words in Matthew 28:19-20,

> *Go therefore and make disciples of all the nations, baptizing them in the name of the Father and the Son and the Holy Spirit, teaching them to observe all that I commanded you; and lo, I am with you always, even to the end of the age.*

Did you catch Jesus' last promise? It is the greatest! "I am with you always . . .!" Disciple-making is not glamorous, hard to quantify, and demands time, BUT produces fruit beyond our expectations, life-change that leads to maturity, and seeks to leave a legacy of generations that live their lives to glorify God. So where do we begin to make disciples? Chapter 8 will offer an example of how you and I can begin to make disciples.

CHAPTER 8
A Plan to Make Disciples

In introducing a plan, I need to make the disclaimer that there is no cookie cutter way to make disciples. Everyone is unique therefore every disciple making initiative is unique. Programs are cookie cutter. Disciple making is not. As was discussed in the previous chapter, a disciple making plan should be centered on the clear goals of making much of Jesus and replication. The disciple maker should also seek to apply wisdom. Specifically, invest in those who are F.A.T., maximize impact by meeting with two people versus one, and key their focus on fruit for the kingdom. Fundamentals of disciple making are solid and necessary. Wisdom dictates that in order to achieve success you must have a plan. Proverbs 21:5 states,

> *The plans of the diligent lead surely to advantage, But everyone who is hasty comes surely to poverty.*

But beyond these principles, I think that there can be much creative implementation within disciple making. Disciple making is not, and even resists programming. As I look back, I wonder where I learned to meet with men, engage them in spiritual disciplines, and challenge them to make disciples. I did not learn disciple making from a program or a book though there are programs and books that have been informative. I did not learn disciple making from a workshop, conference, or class though these can be beneficial. I learned to make disciples from watching the lives of disciple makers as they invested in me.

In seminary I had the privilege of taking a hermeneutics class with Dr. Howard Hendricks. "Prof" as we called him was a godly man with an incredible gift for teaching. I never missed a class and loved his teaching, but it was not his teaching that had the profoundest impact on my life. It was his example.

As Prof would passionately teach, he would pause to make asides in the middle of his lecture to impart something of special importance to him. One of his most consistent asides was that he regularly met with twelve men to study the Bible and make disciples. This impressed me! Here was an eighty-two year old man who had his doctorate, raised four children, taught for over fifty years, fought cancer losing an eye (hence his eye patch), and who was still passionate about making disciples. At the same time, I was probably being convicted. Disciple making had been modeled for me and was being modeled by Prof's example. But I had convinced myself that I was too busy to be making disciples.

Author? look.

Howard Hendricks was a man who was being greatly used by God. I wanted to be used by God, too. It was why I quit my job, moved a thousand miles, was struggling through Greek and Hebrew, working as a missionary to pay for our housing, and asking my wife to work to pay for seminary. I wrongly assumed that it was not the time for me to make disciples. In hindsight this was not true, there was one big difference between Prof and myself and it was not the eye patch! When it came to disciple making, Prof had a plan, and I did not.

How can you make disciples? Have a plan. It stands to reason that there are many plans that can be implemented in disciple making. Again, no one-way is the right way, but there are more and less effective ways to make disciples who replicate. In the end, you and I will stand before God as stewards of the time, resources, and gifts, which He has given us. We want to appropriate these talents in a way that glorifies God.

Here are three concepts that I believe must be injected into any plan to make disciples. You can borrow individual pieces from this plan, but I hope you will seriously consider implementing these three aspects of disciple making DNA into your strategy.

Pray Big

Engaging in disciple making can be hard, but we serve a big God. Disciple making is His plan. Disciple making is underwritten through prayer. Pray that God would use you to make disciples. Pray that God would move in the lives of those that you invest in and that they would make disciples. Pray for wisdom as you seek to be a disciple maker.

You may never meet someone who makes disciples. You may have never been challenged to make a disciple. Perhaps no one has ever intentionally invested in you. How can you begin to make disciples? One word, pray!

When I went to Purdue University, I knew I needed to understand better who Jesus was. I had heard stories from my dad of Navigator Bible studies, discipleship, and men and women who made disciples. I knew college was a place where my faith would be challenged. I found the Navigator leader, John, and asked him multiple times during my first months at Purdue to disciple me. At first he blew me off. I think he was seeing if I was F.A.T. or a flake. I kept asking John if he had time to meet and finally, he agreed. We began to pray together, read the Bible, memorize Scripture, ask tough life questions, and share the Gospel. My time investment with John paid off. I grew in my faith. That summer, God began to move in my heart to pray that He would allow me the privilege of making disciples. I am willing to bet that John was praying that I would invest in other men.

The summer of my sophomore year, I prayed Matthew 4:19, "Lord, let me become a fisher of men." Later that summer, an older man named Bruce Craig passed away. Bruce had been a successful banker and in my mind was a spiritual giant. As a child, he had been a pillar in our small church. Men like my father spoke highly of Bruce and sought his counsel. In high school I had helped Bruce clean out his garage. He was downsizing to move into a retirement community. His woodshop sat empty, along with his manicured lawn and empty gardens. We talked while we sorted through his belongings to give away.

While I do not remember exactly what Bruce and I talked about that day, Bruce impressed on me that life was short and all the temporal things he had were now of no use to him. Bruce's wife was in poor health and for the last decade he had lovingly cared for her. About the time I left for college, Bruce's wife died. A year later Bruce died and I was able to attend his church funeral. As I sat on the back row I marveled at how many people were present, there was not an open seat. As the service neared the end, the pastor gave those in attendance the opportunity to share how Bruce had impacted them. For the next thirty minutes, men stood one at a time and shared how Bruce had invested in them. Through tears they shared how Bruce had taken time to point them toward Jesus.

Bruce was a disciple maker. His investment impacted each man differently as husbands, fathers, and leaders in their circles of influence. Bruce's life had not been lived for self; it had been invested in something greater, the lives of men for the sake of the Kingdom. He had made disciples.

I wanted to be like Bruce. I wanted for the sake of Christ to leave a legacy that would outlive me. Through tears, I prayed "Lord, let me invest my life for You in men!" Unknown to me, God was already in motion. A young man named John was beginning to read his Bible, and two months later Bob and I would show up on his doorstep. God wants us to make disciples. We just need to ask Him.

My journey is unique to me. Yours will be unique to you. We need to ask God to allow and help us be disciple makers. Pray specifically. If you need to grow in your faith and better know what it means to be a disciple of Jesus, ask God to connect you with someone with a passion for disciple making who would invest in you. You can always ask someone you respect to invest in you. Remember to be persistent. If you are following Jesus and want to make disciples, pray that God would give you two men (or two women, if a woman) that you can begin to invest in.

Peggy had called to process some life circumstances. As we closed the conversation, I prayed for her and then asked, "Peggy, have you ever thought about investing in some younger ladies? "Yes, I've actually been praying that God would use me in greater ways," she responded. I recommended that she read through the book of John with two ladies over five or six weeks and invest in their lives. Two weeks later, she excitedly caught me in the hall and shared how the Lord had brought to mind two younger ladies and they had agreed to meet. Two months later, I asked her about her time with the ladies. "Wonderful," she responded. She had prayed. God had answered.

I'm not sure Peggy had ever been exposed to disciple making, but God engaged her in it. Not everyone has seen intentional disciple making that leads to spiritual reproduction (disciples who make disciples). Peggy was unique in that she did have a pastor who helped her connect the disciple making dots. Yet this was not my experience, I saw disciple making modeled by my dad. He was not a pastor, but almost thirty years prior to my prayers he also prayed that he would be a man who made disciples. In a sense, Peggy as a disciple maker is a spiritual granddaughter of my dad's. You want to make disciples, tell God. He will keep His promises. You just have to ask.

What if you do not have a pastor or a dad to help you? I have good news for you. Jesus is the biggest fan of disciple making. As a follower of Jesus, you have access to Him. He has all power. Pray and let Him connect the disciple making dots.

Take the Initiative

Do not just pray, but take the initiative. Once you have prayed, invite two others to join you as you seek to grow in your faith. Choose people from the "as you are going" areas of your life. You are already connected to many through the natural ebb and flow of your life. Pause and take a minute to think through who God has placed in your life. The "as you are going" relationships that God has placed in your life could also be called, life circles.[67]

What does initiative look like in more detail? Three things: choose two individuals to meet with, set expectations for your time together, and be a facilitator.

(1) **Choose two individuals** that are serious about their faith and appear to be hungry to follow Jesus. Pick people out of your life circles. These people must be F.A.T. (faithful, available, or teachable) or your initiative will be frustrated. If you are looking and praying, the Lord will bring people to mind.

1. Once you identify two individuals, approach them and ask if they would pray about meeting together once a week for five to six weeks to read through a book of the Bible like John, memorize Scripture, pray for each other, and encourage each other to be like Jesus and make disciples.

2. Most likely they will say yes, but if they are hesitant it may be due to the current busyness of their calendar. If they say yes, calendar a date and time, pick a place to meet, and communicate what the expectation for the first meeting date will be.

3. Before the first meeting, encourage

and remind those you are meeting to read through the passages while asking two questions of each chapter or paragraph: (1) who is Jesus; that is, who does He claim to be? and (2) How does this impact my life?[68]

(Handwritten notes in margin: "1) who does he say he is? 2) How does it do")

I had wanted to meet with Travis as he was a natural leader, committed church member, and a Sunday School teacher. Every fall, spring, and summer I seek to meet with men and I try to launch as many disciple making groups as there are available F.A.T. people. I always ask Travis, but he had never been available. Travis has a daughter in college and a son who is a gifted high school athlete. Travis had been unavailable, but I continued to ask and finally caught him during a window between sports seasons. After we finished the book of John before Christmas, I asked if he would like to continue after the New Year through the book of James. He was not available in the spring because of sports schedules. I appreciated Travis's honesty and said I would circle back with him in the summer. He agreed and thanked me for taking the initiative to invest in him. It is important to be sensitive to life circumstances. Just because an individual cannot meet one season, does not necessarily mean that they do not want to meet in another season.

(2) **Set the expectations** for the study a week before you meet and then send a reminder two-three days before the meeting time. I typically like to go through the book of John

first followed by the book of James. I ask each member of the group to read through the first five chapters of John and memorize John 3:30 for our first meeting. As individuals walk through the book on their own during the week, they ask two questions: "Who is Jesus or who is God?" and "So what?" I will consistently stress the importance of consistency in the Word and ask guys to be in the Word 4-5 times a week.

I like going through the book of John because it focuses on Jesus from heaven down while the synoptic Gospels look at Jesus from earth up. John has the seven "I am" statements as well as seven unique interactions with individuals who came face to face with Jesus. Because of this the book of John works really well with the questions: who is Jesus and so what? While many have heard the Gospels preached in small sections, most have never walked through a Gospel quickly to get a good understanding of the narrative. James is a great second book because it teaches the Bible student to sink down into a book. Each week you focus on one chapter reading the chapter multiple times. James also is a very straight-forward book that is very black and white in nature and offers lots of wisdom. James is actually called the, "Proverbs of the New Testament."

Here is how both the books of John and James break down over a 5-6 week meeting period.

The Gospel of John breaks down into five weeks likes this:

Week:	Passage:	Memory Verse: *
Week 0	Initial meeting used to introduce the plan.	
Week 1	John 1-5	John 3:30
Week 2	John 6-9	John 6:35
Week 3	John 10-13	John 12:25
Week 4	John 14-17	John 14:21
Week 5	John 18-21	John 13:34-35

*I like to also memorize the Romans Road (3:23, 6:23, 5:8, 10:9-10, 10:13) one verse a week, alongside one verse out of John. This means two verses a week. Most will balk at this but with a little encouragement by you and discipline by them; they will succeed.

The book of James breaks down into five weeks like this:

Week:	Passage:*	Memory Verse:
Week 0	Initial meeting used to introduce the plan.	
Week 1	James 1	Pick verse from c. 1.
Week 2	James 2	Pick verse from c. 2.
Week 3	James 3	Pick verse from c. 3.
Week 4	James 4	Pick verse from c. 4.
Week 5	James 5	Pick verse from c. 5.

*Read the chapter weekly 4-5 times and attempt to read the whole book in one sitting once a week.

Other books of the Bible:

Almost any book in the Bible can be read in one of these two formats. The Gospels, Genesis, Exodus, 1-2 Samuel, and 1-2 Kings, and Acts are all narratives (stories) which can be read like the book of John in chunks. Books such as the prison epistles (Titus, 1 and 2 Timothy) and other Pauline Epistles (Galatians, Ephesians, Philippians, Colossians) can be read like the book of James by "soaking" in the shorter chapters.[69]

I find books such as Romans, Hebrews, and the Corinthians that cover broad theological, historical, or complex cultural contexts or more confusing books such as the Minor Prophets or books that are apocalyptical (Daniel, Ezekiel, and Revelations) are better reserved for a teaching or a self-study context with the aid of a trusted commentary or quality Bible teacher. If you have invested in a group over a long time and they are theologically ready to tackle these books, do not shy away. "All Scripture is God breathed and is profitable . . ." (2 Timothy 3:16).

Lastly, when I want to shift gears or need to take a break from meeting around major holidays on the calendar or seasonal transitions in life, I will choose to read through Proverbs for a month (31 days ~ 31 Proverbs) or encourage those that I am meeting with to spend some time in the Psalms on their own while still picking verses to memorize. At the end of the month, we come back together to discuss the book and review verses and then jump into another five to six weeks of studying a book together.

(3) **Guide**, do not lead a meeting or teach a study, facilitate a conversation. Disciple making is not a board meeting. Disciple making is not a class-room lecture. Disciple making is not hearing from the sage on the stage. Disciple making is better described as facilitating, partnering, or possibly quarterbacking. You are not trying to be the expert but instead impart a love for Jesus while modeling disciple making so that it can be replicated. You do not need to be the teacher or the expert. When you come together to meet, each member of the group has done the same amount of study in God's Word, all have asked the same questions, and all are pursuing Jesus. You are there to encourage, guide, and facilitate.

Here are eight practices that I have identified that are helpful to me in order to facilitate disciple making groups. While these practices work for me, they may not work for you.

1. I like to **meet early in the day**. Breakfast or maybe lunch. Most live busy lives with responsibilities both at work and at home. For most the morning is the best part of their day as they have not faced the challenges and pressures of their day which tend to run them down. It is definitely the best part of my day so I give my best to disciple making. While meeting

early is not the only time that you can meet, it has merit. Some may need to meet on a lunch break or after the kids go down for a nap. For others, evenings may work best.

2. Because people are busy, I like to **meet around food**, while this is not the purpose of our time together, it makes the environment more inviting and relaxed. It also allows busy people to kill two birds with one stone. All have to eat. Jesus did some of His greatest teaching around food. Food changes the atmosphere and feels more like fellowship than formality. Food makes people relaxed.

3. **Pray** at the beginning and the end of the meeting. If those you are meeting with are young in the faith, this is an excellent opportunity for them to listen to you pray and practice praying in a safe environment. As you are leaving, have each in the group share a prayer request and then encourage all to pray for each other during the week. If time permits, pray for each other or have all pray for the man on his right or his left. Be creative. Boring prayer goes stale fast.

4. **I verbalize that my intended goal in**

meeting together is to prepare men to make disciples who make disciples. This may be quite a leap for some. But I find that if I do not set this expectation in the first or second meeting then it just does not happen! I ask both men, even though they may not be clear what they are getting into, to begin praying that God would be working in the lives of two men who they can meet with in the future.

5. I only **ask for a short-term commitment**. Some may disagree with this decision, but it works well in the context I find myself living and ministering. I take 5-6 week runs depending on the book that we are studying. This is very intentional. First, people are really busy and will often balk at a 12 or 15-week study. Five to six week cycles seem to fit the rhythm of life that most people lead. Secondly, while I only ask for short-term commitments, I have found that F.A.T. people will keep coming back for more 5-6 week runs. Over time a consistent pattern of short runs becomes more long-term in nature. One other thought. A short- term run, keeps me honest as the disciple maker. I cannot assume that I or the man across from me will be afforded the

privilege of a long-term disciple making relationship. Remember Scott who moved to Seattle, we only had a few weeks together. This means that I must not waste the time. Thirdly, a short run gives me opportunity to reassess. If one of the two participants does not consistently show up, there is a natural seam to onboard a replacement. Also, if a man is not F.A.T., I can gently release him from the group and avoid awkwardness or hurt. The conversation might go something like this:

"Hey, Bob thanks for meeting with me. We are going to take a break for a while, maybe we can read through another book in the future. Let me know when you think you have the time to do this again and we'll see if our calendars sync." If Bob has consistently not been reading the Word, memorizing his verse, or living in sin, he will breathe a huge sigh of relief that you are letting him off the hook. If he has not dropped out already then the only reason that he has stayed in the group is because he does not want to lose his relational equity with you. Your releasing him at a natural seam is a way for him to save face. If at any time, Jesus moves in his life and Bob becomes F.A.T., then you can pick him up again.

6. If I read through a second book with an individual, I **ask them to write out their one-page testimony**. I also ask

them to share their testimony for five minutes at the beginning of one of our meeting times. This is a great way to get to know each other and will help your group to bind tighter. Hearing a believer's unique testimony is both encouraging and creates a greater sense of openness and vulnerability.

I like to **have each member of the group facilitate** our meeting during our second book study. This allows for a platform to practice facilitating a small group meeting in a safe context. After an individual has facilitated, I will circle back with him and ask two questions: (1) what is one thing you felt you did well as you facilitated and (2) what is one thing that you will do differently the next time you facilitate? These two questions will help the individual self-assess and grow in his ability to facilitate.

7. These discipleship groups are **not designed to be accountability groups** but disciple making groups. Yet, the longer you meet together the more comfortable you will become with each other and the more you will share out of your lives. These groups can easily be tailored to incorporate aspects of accountability as the needs

of the group dictate. Accountability takes time and often takes away from the focus on the Word. I would encourage you to keep the Word and Jesus at the center of your discussion. If greater accountability is desired, I would consider asking group members to touch base at another time during the week to focus on accountability questions. Both accountability and disciple making are great things and have considerable overlap. You as the facilitator will need to decide what the desired purpose of the group will be. I prefer to keep it simple and stay focused on disciple making.

8. Once I have met with a group for two or three 6-week runs, I like to **cut men loose** to try to facilitate a group for themselves. I may offer to meet with them once or twice while they are meeting with their group to play the part of cheerleader and consultant. Once they have proven willing to fish for men and lead a group on their own, I will often sign up for another 6-week run with these men to invest in them again while helping them process through their first experience. This not only allows me to invest in them more, but also allows them to learn in a deeper way after having attempted to

facilitate a disciple making group for themselves.

Commit to a Journey of a Lifetime

Disciple making is not a program. It is a relationship with a purpose. You do not have to have a nifty name or a slick flier to do disciple making. You can call what you are doing whatever you want to: a John-James study group, disciple making, coaching, facilitating, chasing Jesus, coming alongside, encouraging, mentoring, or whatever other name suits your purpose. The name is a detail. The outcome is a movement.

Disciple making is not a program. It is a lifelong journey. You may meet with an individual for five weeks like my friend who moved to Seattle. God may give you an extended season like the five years I was privileged to be with John. You may meet three times: spring, summer, and fall and cover three books of the Bible. Disciple making is not a rushed job or a checked box. God will give you wisdom. The goal is to see those that you invest in become more like Jesus, spread their wings and make disciples who can make disciples. So how do you and I make a disciple? We need a plan. We need a plan that involves prayer, initiative, and engagement in the journey of a lifetime.

Disciple making takes effort, but it is not complex. Disciple making always leads to reproduction. There are many great things that we can do for the

Kingdom, but let us be brutally honest about what we have and have not accomplished.

Disciple making is hard, but it is beautifully simple. Do not chase nice guys; you will quit disciple making. Identify men and women who are hungry to chase Jesus. Pray for men and women who are F.A.T. and you will be addicted to disciple making.

Disciple making is hard. Why bother with disciple making? We make disciples because rain or shine, many or few, good or bad – Jesus is worthy. The only enduring and worthy motive for disciple making is Jesus.

Read once again, the words of Jesus to us His disciples,

> I have been given all authority in heaven and on earth. Therefore, go and make disciples of all the nations, baptizing them in the name of the Father and the Son and the Holy Spirit. Teach these new disciples to obey all the commands I have given you. And be sure of this: I am with you always, even to the end of the age.[70]

All authority has been given to Jesus.
Jesus commands you and me to make disciples.
Jesus promises He will be with us.

Tuesday morning I will wake up early to meet with two men and by God's grace obey Jesus' command to make disciples. I approached these men the week before and asked if they were willing to meet with me. I set the expectations up front. We will read through the book of James. We will memorize a verse each week. We will commit to be in the Word in preparation during the week. No one is teaching, but I am guiding. We will eat breakfast, pray, and talk about the ultimate goal of replicating. We will meet for six weeks, write out our testimonies, take turns facilitating, and (when they are ready) go find other men to start three new groups.

I have been praying for both of these men this week that their time in God's Word would be rich, and that they would continue to grow in Jesus. I pray that they will replicate. I pray that other men and women in my church will catch the vision for making disciples who reproduce. I also pray bigger prayers. I pray that God would continue to bring faithful, available, and teachable men across my path in whom I can intentionally invest for the sake of Jesus. I pray there will be a day when I can go into any restaurant in my small town and find three others circled around the Word of God. I pray that God would multiply my small efforts in great ways and allow me to make disciples in every nation in the world.

I am trying to take Jesus' command to make disciples seriously. I have identified two men. I have a plan. I am using it.

What's your plan to make disciples? Will you join me? Will you make disciples?

ACKNOWLEDGMENTS

There are several thank yous that I would be remiss to not include at the conclusion of this book. First, thanks to my dad and mom, Rick and Cindy Kramer. Your hearts to both serve Jesus and make disciples, have and continue to be godly examples for me.

Second, after almost seven years of pastoral ministry together, there has been no one who has greater influenced my heart for evangelism and missions than Pastor Sammy. Three mission trips to Africa sharing Jesus in the slums of Kampala, follow-ups on the front porch of a church visitor's home with the intention to share the Gospel, identifying and praying for my "top-five" lost friends, and the personal goal of sharing the Gospel once a week have all been influenced by Pastor Sammy's heart for the lost. These have all stretched me to follow Christ in greater obedience to His commands (Acts 1:8). For Pastor Sammy, I am probably one of many who have influenced his thinking on disciple making. But in the last seven years, I have watched as he has placed a greater and greater value on disciple making which has culminated in the commissioning of this book. Pastor Sammy's disciple making efforts have been both broad and deep through training endeavors such as the training of mission teams, investing heavily in men who are now planting churches in St. Louis and

Indianapolis, prioritizing the facilitating of lunch time disciple making groups in the midst of his very full calendar, and he has graciously paved the way (and in some seasons pushed) for me to invest focused time and wiser practices in disciple making activities for the sake of the church.

A special thanks needs also to be given to three other individuals for three different reasons. First, thank you to Dr. Pettegrew who read the early versions of this book, gave me an A, and graciously suggested that I take off some rough edges. Second, thank you to Mrs. Debbie, "the muscle," behind this operation. Thank you for your tireless work editing, polishing, and publishing. Third, thanks to my beautiful bride, Katherine. My first great paring of this life, my most honest and loving critic, who has read every word I have written and been my constant source of encouragement in times of doubts and discouragement in both life and ministry. Words fail to express my gratitude. We share much in life. One of the first characteristics that attracted me to you and runs even deeper and wider now was your heart for disciple making fueled by a love for Jesus. I love you, Babe!

NOTES

[1]John's last name has been omitted for the sake of mission work in closed countries.

[2]In the original language, the only imperative (or command) in Matthew 28:19-20 is "make disciples."

[3]The term Great Commission (Matthew 28:19-20) has often been referred to as the Great Omission. While this may seem to be an unfair critique, this survey speaks to the validity of the statement. Research Releases in Faith & Christianity, March 27, 2018, https://www.barna.com/research/half-churchgoers-not-heard-great-commission/, accessed May 1, 2018.

[4]It is worth noting that many Bible translations create a parallel between Mark 16:15 and Matthew 28:19-20 in part by applying a header "The Disciples Commissioned" to Mark 16:15. While the weight of Mark 16:15 seems to align more with Acts 1:8, the weight of Matthew 28:19-20 is directed toward disciple making. Yet, even with this observation, evangelism and disciple making are not mutually exclusive. They are inclusive. Evangelism is a necessary part of disciple making.

[5]Sometimes as Pastors we see our primary tool for disciple making as being our responsibility to preach.

[6]"Dynamics of Church Planting Movements: Lessons from History," accessed February 4, 2018, https://noplaceleftworldcom.files.wordpress.com/2016/02/move ment-models-wesley-whitefield.pdf, 2-3.

[7]What does it look like to accept Jesus as Savior? We must believe (trust, place our faith in the fact) that Jesus Christ is the Son of God, died for our sin, was buried, and rose again. If we accept Jesus as our Savior from our sins, we then receive a restored relationship with God and eternal life with Him.

[8]All three of these initiatives are Biblical and should be normative in the Christian life. The Bible clearly speaks to these three initiatives. Engage in church – Hebrews 10:24-25. Read the Bible and Pray – Hebrews 4:12 and 1 Peter 5:7. Share the Gospel - Romans 1:16 and Acts 1:8.

[9]While not all disciples know their specific spiritual gift, Disciple 2.0 actively seeks to engage with the church through serving. Spiritual gifts have been designed for the Church, and it is within the context of Church that spiritual gifts are exercised (for further study, see 1 Corinthians 12:1-11).

[10]If you are a pastor reading this book and wondering how to fit disciple making into your already overflowing schedule, consider carving out 5-10% of your time to disciple making. A little intentional time invested toward disciple making will go a long way.

[11]It is important to recognize that Jesus' intentional spiritual investment extended beyond Jesus' own family and His synagogue. Our scope for disciple making should not be limited to our family and closest friends.

[12]John Calvin also made disciples. Most present day Reformed denominations trace their roots to Calvin's influence. The Moravians made disciples, too – John Wesley and Charles Wesley influenced George Whitefield. John Wesley had a holiness club in college, a group of men that met together specifically to pursue Jesus, and when it was coupled with his mother's influence and his interaction with the Moravians, Methodism was born.

[13]It is said that Wesley and Whitefield single-handedly kept England from descending into bloodshed as France marched

many off to the guillotine.

[14]The validity of this statement by Moody has recently been debated; but pastoral lore will continue to faithfully proclaim and where the shoe fits, wear it (Moody was a shoe salesman). Mark Fackler, "The World Has yet to See . . ." (Christianity Today Issue 25: Dwight L. Moody: 19th Century Evangelist), http://www.christianitytoday.com/history/issues/issue-25/world-has-yet-to-see.html, accessed May 5, 2017.

[15]While disciple making relationships don't necessarily have to be a father-son or mother-daughter relationship, these relationships are full of potential both for modeling and teaching. Parents, like none other, have the opportunity to model their faith to their children.

[16]Disciple making doesn't happen through osmosis. Disciple making may not be a program, but it requires a plan. Daniel Wallace gives a convincing argument that the participle "go" bears the weight of the imperative because of its placement of priority at the beginning of the sentence. Dan Wallace, The Great Commission or the Great Suggestion, https://danielbwallace.com/tag/matthew-2819-20/, accessed May 3, 2018. This argument aligns well with the intentionality of disciple making.

[17]Works such as Bill Mowry's *The Way of the Alongsider: Growing Disciples Life to Life,* are excellent resources for a disciple maker to walk alongside a disciple and can be used in any context.

[18]The simplest and clearest definition of disciple making that I have seen is the Mission Statement of the Navigators: "To know Christ and make Him known."

[19]The context of this 5th reason to make disciples is important to acknowledge. We live in a highly "me" centered culture, which often bleeds into the church. The ideals of the American dream, the pursuit of material possessions, and the longing for comfort tend to feed self-impulses. The attitude of "what is in it for

me?" is a safe place to be, but Jesus calls us beyond a self-centered existence of comfort and ease to a life of sacrifice, decrease, and living for the sake of others.

[20] An excellent Biblical example of this can be seen in the generation of Israelites that followed Joshua.

[21] Taken from an e-mail discussion with my father, Rick Kramer; April 6, 2018.

[22] In John 13:34-35, Jesus gives the mark of His disciples as love for one another.

[23] There will always be blessing found in maturity, but not necessarily material blessing. Jesus calls us to "hate" (John 12:25) and "lose" (Matthew 10:39) this life. He also promises that He will meet our needs (Philippians 4:19, Matthew 6).

[24] The Westminster Catechism asks the question, "What is the chief end of man?" The answer, "The chief end of man is to love God and glorify Him forever." One of the ways we glorify God in this life is to make disciples, who love God and glorify God with their lives."

[25] The following example of Apple Computers comes from *Start with Why* by Simon Sinek. Simon Sinek, *Start with Why: How Great Leaders Inspire Everyone to Take Action* (New York, Portfolio, 2011).

[26] If this were not the case, we have cause for great concern. Take for instance the Jehovah's Witnesses. There are 8.3 million Jehovah's Witnesses involved in evangelism activities. Jehovah's Witnesses are not practicing relational evangelism over coffee. They show up at your doorstep trying to convert you to their faith ("cold turkey evangelism"). To put this into context there are roughly 16 million on the rolls in the Southern Baptist Convention (the largest evangelical denomination in the United States). The reality is that on average there are 5.5 million Southern Baptists in church on a given Sunday. This

means there are more Jehovah's Witnesses knocking on doors than Southern Baptists in the pews on Sunday. If you are Southern Baptist, this statistic might be cause for concern, but the real question is are Jehovah's Witnesses making disciples that last?

[27]The Church is designed to edify the believer (Ephesians 4:12). Organizations make poor disciples. People make disciples. The primary commission of pastors is to equip the saints for the work of ministry (Ephesians 4:12), preaching (2 Timothy 4:2), and shepherd the flock (1 Peter 5:2). As followers of Jesus, pastors are to make disciples, which includes evangelizing the lost.

[28]Barna, in its recently commissioned study for the Navigators and NavPress, stated,

> The research examined the language and terminology surrounding discipleship. We asked a random sample of Christians—including practicing and non-practicing Christians—what words or phrases they use to describe "the process of growing spiritually." The most preferred term was "becoming more Christ-like" (selected by 43% of respondents), followed by "spiritual growth" (31%), and "spiritual journey" (28%).

> The term "discipleship" ranked fourth on the list and was only selected by fewer than one in five Christians (18%). "Spiritual maturation" was next (16%). "Sanctification" (9%) and "spiritual formation" (5%) were relatively unused phrases among the general population of Christians.

> Interestingly, the more active the person in spiritual activities, the more likely he or she is to use the phrase "becoming Christ-like." In contrast, the "spiritual journey" language is most preferred among non-practicing Christians.

"New Research on the State of Discipleship, by David Kinnaman, Barna Research, December 1, 2015; https://www.barna.org/research/leaders-pastors/research-release/new-research-state-of-descipleship#.V2W4ps6c9UQ, accessed June 18th, 2016.

[29]Dietrich Bonhoeffer, *Life Together: The Classic Exploration of Christian Community.*

[30]It is also ironic that Barna in studying the terminology surrounding discipleship chose to use "the process of growing spiritually" as the descriptive factor for discipleship.

[31]Ibid.

[32]My title was later changed to Discipleship Pastor.

[33]Ed Stetzer writes in the forward to *Rediscovering Discipleship* by Robby Gallaty, "41% of American Protestant churchgoers do not attend small classes or groups from their churches." (Gallaty, *Rediscovering Discipleship*, 12).

[34]You may be thinking, "but his son was making a disciple of his grandson so was not this pastor successful?" True, but the son (now a dad) believed that his dad was too busy and distracted by ministry to invest in him!

[35]Brad Waggoner expounds on the concept of discipleship vs. disciple making in his work, *The Shape of Faith to Come: Spiritual Formation and the Future of Discipleship*, 2008.

[36]*Most Christians Want to Be Better Disciples. They Just Don't Know How to Get There.* Bob Smietana, Facts & Trends, (Lifeway, Sothern Baptist Convention 2016), 21.

[37]Transformational Discipleship Assessment; tda.lifeway.com. Waggoner, *The Shape of Things to Come*, 69.

[38]"Churchgoers Believe in Sharing Faith, Most Never Do," by Jon D. Wilke; http://www.lifeway.com/Article/research-survey-sharing-christ-2012; accessed July 15, 2016. See also *Transformational Groups* by Ed Stetzer and Eric Geiger.

[39]For more on the impact of church programming see Willow Creek's excellent research – "Reveal: where you are," by Greg Hawkins and Cally Parkinson.

[40]Tommy Kiker, *Everyday Ministry*, 74-75.

[41]"The Measure of a Ministry," by Chris Adsit, *Discipleship Revolution*(Jan-Feb,2011); http://www.missionfrontiers.org/issue/article/the-measure-of-a-ministry, (accessed July 25, 2016).

[42]*Table 1*, Ranking of Factors Sought for in a Pastoral Candidate (Dallas Seminary's Placement Office). From PM103 Expository Preaching I Notes, page 5, Timothy S. Warren, June 2003. Not reflected in the table below: "Extracurricular," 1.88, Not So Important and "GPA," 1.84, Not So Important.

Preaching Ability	3.74	Very Important
Personal References	3.24	Important
Ministry Experience	3.13	Important
Marital Status	2.99	Important
Age	2.43	Fairly Important
Secular Work Experience	2.36	Fairly Important
Missionary Internship	2.29	Not So Important
Children	2.17	Not So Important

[43]Confucius declared, "I see and I forget, I hear and I remember, I do and I understand."

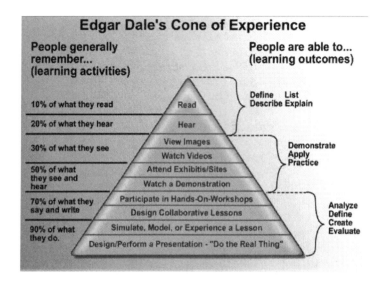

E. Dale, Audiovisual Methods in Teaching, 1969, NY: Dryden Pres.

[45]This taxonomy developed by Dr. Benjamin Bloom, an American educational psychologist, was designed to promote higher forms of thinking in education, such as analyzing and evaluating concepts, processes, procedures, and principles, rather than just remembering facts (rote learning).

[46]To take a page from the fictional 19th century Irish bartender, named Mr. Dooley, who has been credited with the statement, "The job of the newspaper is to comfort the afflicted and afflict the comfortable" (Finley Dunne, *Observations by Mr. Dooley*, 1902). Preaching is to comfort the afflicted and afflict the comfortable.

[47]This man had been tremendously successful and respected in his line of work for 25 years where he dealt almost exclusively with people. He demonstrates tremendous skills in being "people-savvy" and has a diverse background and lots of people experience. He spent four years in the military, has a colorful background before coming to Christ, has faithfully walked with Christ for decades, and it appears that the Lord is preparing him for a new season of service in ministry.

[48]"New Research on the State of Discipleship, by David Kinnaman, Barna Research, December 1, 2015; https://www.barna.org/research/leaders-pastors/research-release/new-research-state-of-descipleship -.V2W4ps6c9UQ, accessed June 18th, 2016.

[49]"New Research on the State of Discipleship, by David Kinnaman, Barna Research, December 1, 2015; https://www.barna.org/research/leaders-pastors/research-release/new-research-state-of-descipleship#.V2W4ps6c9UQ, accessed June 18th, 2016.

[50]"Along-sider" is a term coined by Bill Mallory, see *The Way of the Along-sider* (NavPress, Colorado Springs, CO, 2016).

[51]Basically a participle is a verb with "ing" on the end.

[52]In Greek grammar, the placement of specific words such as nouns, verbs, and participles within the sentence structure bear special importance or emphasis. The reader of the original text would have understood that the placement of the participle "go" at the beginning of the sentence was not a mistake but intended to draw attention to the priority of the word "go" above the other participles "baptizing" and "teaching." The placement of "go" at the front elevates the importance or priority of the action.

[53]Randy Frazee, *Making Room for Life: Trading Chaotic Lifestyles for Connected Relationships*, 50.

[54]I would argue that social media is not the best medium by which to make disciples. Most agree that social media will never replace face-to-face interactions where we can have our voice heard, face seen, and the ability to give a hug or shake a hand. As technology advances, face-to-face interactions where our voices can be heard and faces can be seen are becoming more normative. The Apostle Paul had never been to the church in Rome when he penned his magnum opus to the Romans. We still read, study, and preach the book of Romans today. Social media can be a powerful medium for disciple making, but life-on-life interaction through social media has its limits.

[55]Jim Collins, *Good to Great: Why Some Companies Make the Leap...And Others Don't*, 1 edition (New York, NY: HarperBusiness, 2001).

[56]An excellent biblical example of this is the rich young ruler. Jesus called him to be a disciple, but he did not follow. Many are attracted to Jesus, but few will follow him. Perhaps the most amazing part of the story is that even though the rich young ruler failed to follow, Scripture says that Jesus loved him. We are to love everyone; but we are to intentionally invest in the few who will faithfully follow.

[57]This line of reasoning originates from Dietrich Bonhoeffer in his book *Life Together: The Classic Exploration of Christian Community.*

[58]Bible studies can be found in Sunday School, small groups, affinity groups, and life groups. Bible studies like these typically require a gifted or skilled teacher to lead the group, which makes these groups challenging to replicate because they are dependent on an additional gifted leader or in some case leaders in order to replicate. Bible studies also rarely replicate on their own; these groups naturally form communities that become tight knit and resist giving birth or dividing for the sake of replicating. Many of these groups become closed to outsiders as strong relational bonds form. This means that replication typically requires a good deal of oversight and energy. In

contrast, disciple making doesn't depend on a gifted leader or a skilled teacher, and therefore is prime to replicate on its own. Replication is the lifeblood of disciple making, so while strong relational bonds form they are not designed to overshadow the purpose of the group, replication.

[59]E.M. Bounds, *The Complete Works of E. M. Bounds on Prayer* (Grand Rapids, MI: Baker Books, 1990), 370.

[60]See https://www.barna.com/research/bible-reading-2017-new-years-resolution/ or Russ Rankin's article: "Study: Bible Engagement in Churchgoers' Hearts, Not Always Practiced, http://www.lifeway.com/Article/research-survey-bible-engagement-churchgoers, accessed June 7, 2017.

[61]Charles Haddon Spurgeon, The Golden Alphabet: Exposition of Psalm 119: 33-40.

[62]Charles R. Swindoll, *Insight for Today: A Daily Devotional – Memorizing Scripture*, September 26, 2015; https://www.insight.org/resources/daily-devotional/individual/memorizing-scripture, accessed June 7, 2017.

[63]This book has argued that replication is at the heart of the Great Commission, that Jesus and His disciples replicated, and that the Christian has been commanded to replicate.

[64]Metrics, numbers, nickels, and noses, are not evil or even unusual. Metrics are a useful tool for an intentional and wise leader, but allowing metrics to be the sole or even primary indicator of a church's health can set a church up for failure. We need to be clear on our goals and our theology. The goal of the believer is to make disciples; Jesus builds His Church.

[65]I am in no way advocating that pastors should not support programming, quit preaching, or stop leading; I am calling them to be intentional to give their best, not the scraps, to disciple making.

[66]Power distance is how a perceived lower ranking individual in a society accepts and expects power to be distributed unequally. The term power distance is often used in psychological and sociological studies in regard to how a society or culture manages inequalities between individuals and individual's perception of these inequalities.

[67]See Randy Frazee, *Making Room for Life.*

[68]I text the men in my group two or three days before our first meeting time. People are busy and often appreciate the reminder.

[69]The first format applied to the book of John is more of a survey of the book. Due to the length of the book (21 chapters) more Scripture is covered each week making it more a survey in nature. The advantage to this format is that the reader (or listener) moves through the book quickly enough to get a grasp of the book instead of taking in bits and pieces of the book over a long time. They catch the plot line. Most evangelical Christians are used to absorbing the Word on a Sunday morning in bite- size chunks that are typically less than a chapter. People appreciate grasping a book in its entirety. They will thank you for guiding them through a book that they likely have never read or understood.

The second format applied to James is more of an immersion into the book. Due to the brevity of the book (five chapters), Scripture can be studied in a repetitious manner as well as in its entirety. This allows the student to really master the book. As your group reads and re-reads chapters, they will begin to grasp with better understanding the author's intended purpose of the book as well as better understand the details of the book. Again, most evangelical Christians have a very minimal Scriptural diet in their daily lives. Immersing, or soaking, in a shorter book of the Bible is a feast for a Bible famished Christian.

[70]New Living Translation (NLT) *Holy Bible*, New Living Translation, copyright © 1996, 2004, 2015 by Tyndale House Foundation.

I ① JOHN ①
II ② JAMES
③ GENESIS
④ Exodus ②
⑤ 1 SAM ④
⑥ 2 SAM ⑤
⑦ 1 KINGS ⑧
⑧ 2 KINGS ⑨
⑨ ACTS
⑩ TITUS ③
⑪ 1 TIM ⑥
⑫ 2 TIM ⑦
13 GAL ⑩
14 EPH ⑪
15 Phil ⑬
16 Col ⑭
17 PROV ⑫ 31 DAYS

⊘ 6:10 → 7:30 ?
TUESDAY'S

70083981R00104

Made in the USA
Columbia, SC
19 August 2019